THE
ULTIMATE
BOOK OF
BUSINESS
CREATIVITY

THE ULTIMATE BOOK OF BUSINESS CREATIVITY

50 GREAT THINKING TOOLS FOR TRANSFORMING YOUR BUSINESS

ROS JAY

CAPSTONE

First published 2000 by
Capstone Publishing Limited
Oxford Centre for Innovation
Mill Street
Oxford OX2 0JX
United Kingdom
http://www.capstone.co.uk

A CIP catalogue record for this book is available from the British Library and the US Library of Congress

ISBN 1-84112-066-9

Typeset in 11 pt Plantin by
Sparks Computer Solutions Ltd, Oxford
http://www.sparks.co.uk
Printed and bound by
T.J. International Ltd, Padstow, Cornwall

This book is printed on acid-free paper

Substantial discounts on bulk quantities of Capstone books are available to corporations, professional associations and other organizations. If you are in the USA or Canada, phone the LPC Group for details on (1-800-626-4330) or fax (1-800-243-0138). Everywhere else, phone Capstone Publishing on (+44-1865-798623) or fax (+44-1865-240941).

Contents

Introduction

"Creativity consists of looking at the same thing as everyone else and thinking something different."

Albert Szent-Gyorgyi
(biochemist and Nobel Prize winner)

"It is the function of creative man to perceive and to connect the seemingly unconnected."

William Plomer (writer)

Everyone has their own definition of creativity, but most of us know it when we see it. Creativity is the first step towards innovation – it is the process of generating ideas, but there is more to it than that. The ideas generated by the creative process must be workable. There is no creative value in an idea which cannot be applied.

The creative function of the mind is not easy to explain. It belongs in the part of the brain which is not logical, rational and analytical, but abstract, intuitive and non-linear. It is no surprise that we often say "an idea came to me" or "it just popped into my mind" – even when you have just had a creative idea, you probably don't really know how you did it. However, creativity is largely about being able to see patterns and connections that you and others had not detected before.

Creativity is about change. Changing the way we look at things, changing the way we do things. As Miles Davis said: "If anyone wants to keep creating, they have to be about change."

The creative culture

Creativity is certainly a skill and not simply a talent you are born with. Although some of us practice it more than others, we can all become creative thinkers with a little training. And creativity is fast becoming an essential skill that we *must* all learn. It is no longer enough to have a few creative people in the organization; you need to have an organization of creative people. The pace of change in business is accelerating, and creative ideas are essential for keeping up with that pace. Businesses around the world – including your competitors – are learning to create a culture of creativity. Organizations like 3M, Hewlett-Packard and Texas Instruments have led the way, but soon creative organizations will be the norm.

So how do you turn your business into a creative organization? First, you need a culture which fosters creativity, and then you need to teach the people in the organization to use their creative ability. Creating the right culture involves:

- encouraging people to use intuitive as well as logical skills;
- rewarding creativity;
- using group creative techniques as a regular approach to problem solving and idea generation; and
- recognizing that creativity isn't possible without mistakes, and therefore allowing mistakes in the pursuit of creativity.

Teaching people to be creative entails showing them techniques, such as the ones in this book, and encouraging them to practice them. As with everything, the more we use our creative skills, the better they become. We can also learn to be creative by imitating others or learning from other people's ideas and approaches. So everyone in the organization should be encouraged to:

- read books which describe other people's creative achievements and inspire new ideas in the reader;
- read newspaper and magazine articles about business successes; and
- network with other people, including visiting on-line support and discussion groups.

It is worth realizing that most creative people do not have a higher quality of ideas than others, so much as a higher quantity. The more ideas you generate, the more good ideas you will generate. Many of the techniques in this book aim to generate a high quantity of ideas for precisely this reason. If you need convincing, here are two illuminating quotes from people who should know what they are talking about:

> "The best way to get a good idea is to get lots of ideas."
> *Linus Pauling (chemist and Nobel Prize winner)*

> "The only sure way to avoid making mistakes is to have no new ideas."
> *Albert Einstein (mathematical physicist and*
> *Nobel Prize winner)*

One study of 2,036 scientists throughout history found that the most highly respected produced not only more great works, but also more bad ones. The point about them was simply that they were prolific.

Thinking in creative mode

While it is almost impossible to describe exactly how you reached a creative realization, there are certain ways of thinking which are more likely to result in creative ideas. Some people divide thinking into two main types:

- *convergent thinking* – logical evaluation to reduce a wide range of ideas or information down to a single answer or idea;
- *divergent thinking* – opening up the mind to produce a wide range of original and diverse ideas.

Both of these have their place, but it is divergent thinking which is the route to creativity. Most of us, however – chiefly through habit – tend to favor convergent thinking most of the time. Convergent thinking is vital to the application of creative ideas, but it is not the way to generate those ideas.

One of the most important methods of divergent thinking is what is often known as lateral thinking (the term coined by Edward de Bono), or "out of the box" thinking. Both of these terms refer to breaking away from narrow, habitual thinking and approaching problems from a different, sideways angle.

For example, suppose you want to phone a friend of yours to ask them to dinner next week, but you don't know the number. You look it up in your address book, but the number you have is out of date. You check the phone book, but they seem to be ex-directory. You call a mutual friend to ask for it, but they are out. You call another and their line seems to be out of order. What do you do? Well, suppose you apply the lateral thinking approach. Don't get hung up on using the phone (if you'll pardon the pun). Why not e-mail them instead? Like most lateral solutions it is blindingly simple once you see it – but for some reason we frequently fail to see these obvious answers.

If the question is right, there must be an answer

It seems that one of the important components of creative thinking is the conviction that there is an answer to your problem. If you know what you are trying to achieve, whether it is understanding the structure of subatomic particles or finding a way to restore your falling sales figures, you need to believe that it is possible. This seems to fire the creative process. Henry Ford said, "Whether you believe you can, or whether you believe you can't, you're absolutely right."

Alexander Graham Bell invented the telephone as a result of a misunderstanding. He read a description of an invention which was written in German. He thought it described an instrument with the function of a telephone so, inspired by this, he developed his own working telephone. He then discovered that the German invention was something else entirely. But his creative ability to invent the telephone had been fired by the belief that it was possible.

Another scientist read about the invention of the electron microscope. He didn't learn, however, the way it worked. So he developed three different ways of building one himself. When he checked the patent, he found that he had duplicated the original discovery with one of his. But, of his remaining two methods, one was superior to the original and made the patent obsolete.

One of the keys to knowing that an answer can be found lies in finding the right question to ask. Bell asked himself how he could create an invention which could relay a voice over distance down a cable, and asking the right question led to his ground-breaking discovery. When asked what single event was most helpful in developing his Theory of Relativity, Einstein replied, "Figuring out how to think about the problem."

To approach a problem using lateral thinking, it often helps to ask yourself, "What am I really trying to achieve here ... and can I achieve it any other way?" In other words, get outside the problem and walk all round it, examining it from different angles. That is how you realize that you are not trying to phone your friend specifically, but simply to communicate with them. Much non-creative thinking is the result of getting stuck in a thinking rut, and devising the right question to ask is often the spur to finding the solution.

Using this book

This book is a collection of recognized, well-used techniques all of which are designed to spark the creative process. A book cannot have your ideas for you, but it can help you to create the right mental environment to have them for yourself. Different techniques suit different problems, and you will find the range of techniques here covers most types of problem you are likely to encounter in business. This book will help you to:

- generate ideas;
- solve complex problems;
- solve simple but seemingly intractable problems;
- create new business opportunities; and
- develop new products and services and improve existing ones.

Once you have become familiar with the techniques here, and incorporated them into your everyday working life, you will find you generate more ideas than you ever had before. Remember, *quantity* of ideas is what counts. You should soon earn yourself a reputation as an ideas person.

I would urge you to try as many of these techniques as you can. If you always use the same one or two, your thinking will get stuck in a rut again – it will just be a different rut from the last one. Each entry explains the type of situation for which that technique is most helpful, so find opportunities to test out something new. You will also find cross-references to other similar or related ideas.

Each entry indicates whether it is generally regarded as an individual or a group technique – but hey, we're being creative here. You can experiment with anything you like; the information here is just a guideline to help you when you first learn the technique. Try using individual techniques in a group, develop your own variations – whatever seems to work. So long as you generate ideas as a result, go for it.

I have also categorized each technique according to whether it is best for problem solving or for idea generation. Clearly you can argue that all idea generation is a form of problem solving, but the point is to try and break down the entries a little so that you can more easily find a technique to suit you. The meaning, for the purposes of this book, of these terms is given below.

- *Problem solving.* You have a specific situation which needs to be resolved (problem) and you need to find ideas to help you achieve this solution (e.g. resolving a design flaw in a product, reducing costs in line with market forces, finding a delivery method that fulfills your cost/quality/time criteria).
- *Idea generation.* You have a broad question which you would like answered, but the need to address it is not so specific (e.g. developing new products, finding new markets, looking for original ways to promote a product or service).

Some techniques are listed as being useful for both applications, and of course you are free to be creative in your use of any of the techniques.

Finally, the matrix shown overleaf may help you to narrow down possible techniques according to whether they are individual or group techniques, and whether they are best for problem solving or idea generation. You should find that most if not all these techniques are not only stimulating but also enjoyable. So relax and have fun – both are states which foster creativity.

In a climate of change, it is creativity which will drive organizations and individuals towards success. And to move forward we must learn – learn to open our minds to new ways of thinking and new possibilities for our organizations, for our products and services, and for ourselves.

> "A learning organization is one that is continually expanding its capacity to create its future. *Survival learning* or what is more often called *adaptive learning* is important – indeed it is necessary. But for a learning organization, *adaptive learning* must be joined by *generative learning*, learning that enhances our capacity to create."
>
> *Peter Senge (academic and author)*

	Problem solving	Idea generation
Individual technique	Analogies and metaphorical thinking Association Attribute listing Conscious intuitive techniques Discontinuity Force-field analysis Involving an outsider Pattern language Problem reversal Questions Random stimulation Sensory images Two words technique Unconscious intuitive techniques Verbal checklist	The 7×7 technique Association Assumption reversal Attribute listing Discontinuity Drawing techniques FCB grid Forced relationship Involving an outsider Lotus blossom technique Mind mapping Morphological analysis Pattern language Random stimulation Sensory images Two words technique Verbal checklist
Group technique	Crawford slip method Delphi technique Excursion technique Gordon/Little technique Nominal group technique Rice storm Six thinking hats Storyboarding Synectics	Brainstorming Brainwriting Drawing techniques Left-brain/right-brain thinking Lotus blossom technique Morphological analysis Rice storm Scenarios Six thinking hats Storyboarding

Matrix of techniques.

The 7 × 7 Technique

T he 7 × 7 technique begins with a large numbers of ideas, each jotted down on a slip of paper. These ideas or thoughts will have been generated in a fairly unstructured way – perhaps through brainstorming, or maybe over a period of time noting down ideas as they come to you. However, they will all be related to a particular objective such as making customers even happier, or restructuring the buying department. In any case, you now have a jumble of ideas and you need to sort them into a logical system so you can address them.

Individual technique: idea generation

This technique for evaluating and prioritizing large numbers of ideas which have been generated in response to a particular objective was developed by Carl Gregory. You start with more ideas than you can get your head around, and you end up with fewer ideas, set out in a structured order of priority.

See also: Storyboarding.

Nine key steps

There are nine key steps in this process (not seven, as you might have imagined). The name of the technique is derived from the fact that you start by setting out your idea slips on a 7 × 7 racking board: one with seven rows and seven columns. (The racking board isn't important; you can lay the slips out anywhere you like.) You are ready to start when you have at least two racking boards full of ideas, or when you have exhausted your pile of idea slips.

Step 1: Combine similar ideas

First, reduce the number of slips by discarding anything which really isn't useful or pertinent. Then combine any duplicated or very similar ideas. Now group together slips of related ideas. You can give each of these groups a collective title.

Step 2: Exclude anything irrelevant

You will no doubt find that some ideas aren't relevant to the objective of the technique, or are completely impracticable. Put these to one side.

Step 3: Modify the ideas

You may now find that some of your remaining ideas need to be modified in the light of the steps you have taken so far.

Step 4: Defer anything which is not timely

You have already excluded ideas which were not relevant. Now you are setting aside ideas which, although relevant to the objective, are not suitable at the moment but may be useful later.

Step 5: Feedback

Check through all the slips you have removed – combined, excluded, modified or deferred – to see if they give you any additional ideas or insights into the remaining slips.

Step 6: Classify into dissimilar columns

Now you've finalized the slips you are using for the rest of the process. The next steps will help you classify and prioritize your ideas. First of all, give each group of related ideas its own column on your racking board. Contrary to what you might imagine, seven columns aren't compulsory for this technique; you may well need a few more.

Step 7: Rank ideas in each column

For each column in turn, rank the ideas in order of the most important or useful – in the context of your objective.

Step 8: Generalize the columns

Give each column a heading which reflects its main theme or idea.

Step 9: Rank the columns

Now put the most important or critical column on the left, the next most important in the next column and so on.

At the end of this process you can easily evaluate which idea is the most important (it's in the top left hand corner), and all your remaining ideas will be prioritized for you with the least important (but still valid) in the bottom right corner.

As you can see, this could just as well have been called the 9 × 9 technique, or the 6 × 8 technique. The precise numbers aren't critical; it is your ideas which matter. Although this technique is essentially an individual one, it can be adapted for use in group sessions.

Example

Let's suppose that your objective is to find ways to make your customers even happier. You've been jotting down ideas for a while, you've held a brainstorming session with key people, and you've asked everyone to pass on any other ideas to you. You have now collected around a hundred or so ideas for improving customer service. However, you clearly can't put them all into effect immediately, so you're going to use the 7 × 7 technique to help you assess and prioritize them.

Combine

To begin with, you can take out redundant idea slips such as *improve despatch method*; you've changed to a far better delivery service since you jotted that one down. And you can combine similar ideas such as *design new catalogue and make catalogue less confusing*.

Exclude

Now set aside the ideas which really aren't on, such as *cut all prices by 50%*.

Modify

You may now find that you want to write out new idea slips in the light of these changes. For example, you could replace the two slips about the catalogue design with only one, which says *design new catalogue with a focus on clarity.*

Defer

This is the time to set aside any slips with ideas which are useful but not right now. For example, *make customer reception area brighter and more modern* can wait until the building is refurbished next year, but will then be worth considering.

Feedback

Some of the ideas you have put aside may give you further useful ideas. Perhaps you *could* cut all your prices by 50% if you did it as part of an offer to new customers, or big spenders, or long-term customers. And maybe you could improve the reception area now if you replaced that tatty old furniture in advance of the refurbishment.

Classify by dissimilar columns

Now put all the ideas you have into related groups. For example, you could create a column out of:

- give more training in customer care;
- increase staffing at busy times;
- give a monthly award to the most customer-friendly member of staff;
- give people from despatch a chance to meet customers;

... and so on: they are all personnel ideas.

Rank ideas in each column

Once you have created your columns, put the ideas in order of importance. Only you know which is the most important, or urgent, but here's an example:

1. increase staffing at busy times;
2. give more training in customer care;
3. give specific training in complaint handling;
4. reward instances of really good customer service by individual staff;
5. give people from despatch a chance to meet customers;
6. give a monthly award to the most customer-friendly member of staff; and
7. put name badges on all staff who meet customers.

Generalize columns

Give a title to each of your columns, for example: people, products, systems, presentation, publications, communications, prices.

Rank columns

Finally, decide what you consider is the most important or urgent column and put it on the left, as shown in the table. Put the remaining columns in order of precedence from left to right.

	systems	products	people	communications	prices	presentation	publications
1							
2							
3							
4							
5							
6							
7							

Analogies and Metaphorical Thinking

T o use this approach to creative problem solving, you first need to know what analogies and metaphors are. An analogy compares two things which are not obviously similar on the surface, but which the analogy shows to be alike in some way. For example, you could explain how white blood corpuscles work by drawing an analogy with a school of piranha fish: they swim around gently until they spot something alien in their environment. They descend on it in a group and attack it until they have destroyed it. Then they go back to floating in the current.

A metaphor is just a simple type of analogy. It is a figure of speech which likewise links two apparently unconnected ideas, such as *the corporate jungle* or *the slings and arrows of outrageous fortune.*

Analogies and metaphors can help you to solve problems creatively by encouraging you to look at your problem from a new angle.

Individual technique: problem solving

Analogies and metaphors are common ways of thinking. This technique harnesses them and uses them to help solve problems by looking at them in a different way.

See also: Forced relationship, Excursion technique, Synectics.

Simply by looking for analogies or metaphors to describe your problem, you often arrive at a solution. All you need to do is to focus on the problem and then think of something else which is basically different but has some similarity. Pursue the comparison and see if it leads you to a solution.

So if your problem is that you intermittently receive so many orders that your despatch department can't process them all, you might decide that this is analogous to everyone trying to get out of a cinema at once when the movie finishes, and having to queue up to leave. A solution to the cinema problem, such as more exit doors, may lead you to a solution to the rush of orders. Perhaps you could have your "exit routes" prepared in advance – stockpile assembled packing cases, do some of the paperwork in advance, service delivery vehicles so none of them is out of action at the crucial time.

The point is partly that forcing yourself to dream up analogies frees you from the kind of logical thinking that stifles many attempts to find a solution to a knotty problem. As you will see when you read the examples below, none of the solutions illustrated would ever have been likely to be reached without the sideways look at the problem that the analogy provided.

Of course not every analogy is guaranteed to lead you to the perfect solution to your problem, and you do have to recognize when you are flogging a dead horse. The whole point about an analogy is that the two ideas are very different although they have similarities. So the comparison will, by definition, break down at some point. And it may break down before reaching a useful answer to your problem.

When this happens, try looking for another analogy. One approach is to list three or four analogies before you start thinking any of them through in detail. If one lets you down, don't worry. Just try the next one. This approach may lead you indirectly to a solution simply by changing the way you think about the problem, even if none of the analogies specifically answers it.

Although this is essentially an individual technique, you will find that it can be used in a group session. Here are some real examples of analogies being used to solve problems.

Example 1

A company making potato crisps wanted to do something to prevent crisp packets taking up so much shelf space. They are filled with air, making them very inefficient in terms of space, but if you remove the air they crumble. The solution lay in an analogy: they decided that crisps were like leaves, and then thought about how you would pack leaves efficiently.

If you compress dried leaves, they break. However, you can press leaves so long as they are moist and not dry. This led the manufacturers to the idea of mixing dried potato with water and then pressing it into shape, so the crisps could be stacked and occupy less space on the supermarket shelves. The resulting product, as you may have guessed, was Pringles.

Example 2

A company in Colorado which manufactured mining equipment wanted to design a machine which could both dig ore and move it onto a conveyor belt. Fortunately, one of the team working on the project was an entomologist, who saw a comparison with a preying mantis, which picks up its food with its forelegs and then puts it in its mouth. This analogy led to the development of a machine which stands astride a conveyor belt and has huge "forelegs" with shovels at the end to dig out the ore and then load it onto the moving belt.

This uses a type of analogy technique known as bionics. It is the same as any other analogous thinking technique, except that you specifically look for analogies in nature.

Example 3

A company which produces farm products wanted to develop a way in which farmers could plant seeds at exactly equal distances apart. Using the analogy of a machine-gun belt, they designed a tape with seeds spaced along it. This could be put in the furrow where the biodegradable ribbon would disintegrate.

Example 4

The modern television was invented in 1921 by a 14 year old boy named Philo T. Farnsworth. He lived on a farm in Idaho, and the neat rows of furrows on the farm gave him the idea of creating a picture out of light and dark dots. As he tilled a potato field with a horse-drawn plough, he conceived the notion of using an electron beam to scan images in the same way. By the age of 21 he had created the first working television which could receive electronic images.

Personal analogy

This is a particular type of technique in which you imagine yourself personally involved in the problem. Suppose you are trying to find a way to improve your supermarket checkouts: imagine that you are an item of shopping being put on the conveyor belt and passed through the checkout. Or you might want to simplify your ordering process: imagine you are an order from a customer and follow your route through the system. The idea is not just to go through the process but to imagine how you would feel in the situation.

Example of personal analogy

In a group personal analogy session at one shampoo manufacturer, the aim was to develop a new shampoo. The managers all imagined that they were human hairs, and considered how they felt being washed. Some wanted to be treated gently, others washed thoroughly. Some hated being blow-dried, others didn't like being washed too often. This wide variation in attitudes led them to realize that hair is different, and they developed a shampoo which could adapt itself to different types of hair. It became one of the top-selling brands.

Association

Most of us have played a game, at least as children, in which one of you says a word. The next person says the first word that comes into their head as a result of hearing the original word, and the next person likewise responds with the first word they think of, and so on. This is called free association, and it is the basis of this creativity technique.

Your mind will generally associate with another word on one of three principles:

- *Contiguity*. This is the principle of an object or idea near to the one mentioned. So the word *encyclopedia* might lead to the word *library*.

Individual technique: problem solving/idea generation

This technique isn't supposed to give you the answer to your question or problem; it is intended to set you on the path towards it. By making associations between things or ideas you can spark off thoughts which lead you to your goal.

See also: Focused-object technique, Forced relationship, Random stimulation, Synectics.

- *Similarity.* Here, you will associate something which is very like the previous word. So *carrot* might follow the word *potato*.
- *Contrast.* In this case, a word opposite or nearly opposite will follow. So *safe* might lead to *dangerous*.

By allowing your mind to associate freely, you can generate thoughts which may spark off useful ideas; this technique aims to generate the spark, not the idea itself. You are simply aiming to create, randomly, a list of words which might help you to look at things differently.

You need to start this process with a word, obviously. You can use a word, or two-word phrase, connected with the issue you want to address, or you can pick a word at random, for example by allowing a book to fall open and pointing at a word on the page where it opens.

Write down your starting word at the top of the page, on the left-hand side. In a column beneath it, write down the next word that comes to mind, and the next, and so on. Keep going until you have a list of around 10–20 words. For example, let's start with the random word seashore:

1. seashore
2. shell
3. cup
4. tea
5. racing car
6. track
7. monitor
8. screen
9. check
10. tartan.

These words are only going to be helpful if you put them into the context of the problem you are trying to solve or the ideas you are trying to generate. So now use the right hand column to note down any thoughts which each of these words gives you in relation to this. For example, suppose you are trying to think of new designs for children's pushchairs, the table might well look as shown:

Word	Free association
Seashore	Design a "four wheel drive" pushchair to push easily on soft or sandy terrain
Shell	Make a rigid weatherproof shell to put the child in which opens out like a clam shell and clicks shut again leaving only the child's head exposed
Cup	Attach a cup or bottle holder to the side of the buggy
Tea	Put a picnic rack on the back which doesn't overbalance the buggy
Racing car	Put a small engine in a pushchair to make going uphill easier
Track	Could the pushchair have caterpillar tracks instead of wheels for pushing on rough ground?
Monitor	Attach a remote tracking device so parents can monitor where nanny takes the pushchair, and which bleeps if it goes out of range
Screen	Incorporate a small television or video screen in front of the child
Check	Design a pushchair which checks whether the safety restraint is done up properly, and won't release the brake unless it is
Tartan	Redesign fabric options in a choice of checks or other patterns

Of course, these words might have sparked off completely different ideas in someone else which is why, although this is generally regarded as an individual technique, it can be very productive as a group technique too.

There are all sorts of variations on the basic free association technique. Here's an example which starts from a phrase related to the issue you want to address. First, you produce a two-word phrase consisting of an action verb and an object. So for the pushchair you might choose the phrase *improve pushchair* or *design seating* or *modify wheels*. You write the words down with four lines drawn between them. Let's use the phrase *adapt buggy*:

Adapt _____   _____   _____   _____ buggy

Now treat the lines as verbal stepping stones, and use free association to get from your starting word to your final word. See if you can give the last of the four words some link to the object, without abandoning the free association.

Adapt   <u>alter</u>   <u>church</u>   <u>service</u>   <u>friendly</u>   buggy

Once again, take each of these words in turn and try to find some way of using them to spark an idea for adapting your buggies:

- *Alter.* Make the height of the handles adjustable to suit whichever adult is pushing.
- *Church.* Create a silent pushchair which won't wake a sleeping baby; no squeaky wheels or creaky seats.
- *Service.* Design a really durable, long lasting buggy which will appeal to parents planning a large family who don't want to keep investing in new pushchairs.
- *Friendly.* Give a buggy a furry lining and arms like a bear's, with paws on the end, and a bear's head above the child's, so they are being hugged every time they sit in it.

Examples

There is no doubt that allowing your mind to pursue a link between two freely associated objects can lead to a creative flash. The popular belief that Newton discovered gravity by being hit on the head by a falling apple was wrong, according to the man himself. His own account of how he conceived the notion of universal gravitation was a little different, and relied on association. The apple certainly fell, though Newton never claimed it hit him on the head; he later said that as the apple fell he simultaneously noticed the moon in the sky. He just happened to associate the moon and the apple in his mind, and to speculate on whether the same force that kept the moon in the sky also made the apple fall.

More recently, Campbell's Soup used free association to develop a new range. Starting with the randomly selected word *handle*, a group free-associated via the word *utensil* to *fork*. Someone made a joke about eating soup with a fork, and the others reflected on the fact that you couldn't possibly eat soup with a fork unless it was full of chunks of meat or vegetables. That's how Campbell's Chunky Soups were conceived.

Assumption Reversal

ere's an assumption that many businesses make: *customers want good service*. But the assumption reversal technique proposes that you turn that around: *customers don't want good service*.

So where did that get us? Well, the point is that by taking a mirror-image view we can generate new ways of approaching problems. And while the reverse assumption itself may not be the answer, it may help to generate an answer. In the example above, try following through the reversal. Suppose you stop giving customers good service; what will happen? Here are a few possibilities:

- You won't need to employ such good staff, or so many of them.
- You won't need to spend so much on staff training.

Individual technique: idea generation

By questioning the seemingly obvious assumptions about a problem, you can spark off new ideas for tackling it. Even the most basic assumptions are up for analysis.

See also: Problem reversal.

- It won't matter if you keep selling out of stock before you've reordered.
- You won't need to personalize mailshots.

These are just a few examples of the effects of not giving customers good service. And you might have noticed that all of them will save you money. Suppose you passed these savings on to the customer? In exchange for good service they will get much lower prices. Or perhaps the answer is to exchange some aspects of good service for a smaller price saving. It's an active policy that has worked very well for some companies. And we only came up with it by reversing the assumption that customers want good service.

Assumption reversal is all about looking at a situation from the opposite perspective. Identify the assumptions you are making and then turn them around. The original assumptions aren't necessarily wrong, but by reversing them you can generate new solutions. Sometimes of course the original assumptions *are* wrong, and false assumptions limit the range of solutions you can come up with. So by breaking the assumptions you widen your scope for resolving your problem.

So what assumptions should you reverse? The answer is, reverse the most basic ones first. Perhaps you want to increase the response to your direct mail campaigns. So start by listing the assumptions you're making. For example, you may be assuming:

- Direct mail is a worthwhile way to promote your products.
- Your products are worth having.
- There is a potential for more response to your mailshots.
- The response you are asking for (call for more information, place an order or whatever) is the one the recipient wants to make.

These are very basic assumptions. But now try reversing them:

- Direct mail is not the best way to promote your products.
- Your products are not desirable to your prospects.
- You are already getting the maximum possible response.

- The recipient doesn't want to respond in any of the ways you are inviting them to.

In some cases the original assumption may have been right, in others it may have been wrong. But either way, this approach should open up new avenues of thought for you. For example:

- Perhaps you should explore the possibility of finding another way to promote your range – advertising or exhibiting or cold calling.
- What would you do if your products weren't good enough? Even if they are, this train of thought may help you improve them. What aspects would need improving or altering? Or is the whole range obsolete – are you doing the equivalent of trying to sell audio cassettes into a market increasingly dominated by CDs?
- What if you have saturated the market, and there are no new customers to reach? It's an unlikely (though not impossible) scenario, but it could lead to some very interesting alternative ideas.
- Suppose you invite a different response to your mailshot. Would prospects like to come to a product demonstration? E-mail a response? Turn up at your exhibition stand?

This example should show you how assumption reversal can open up new lines of investigation that you wouldn't otherwise have explored. When it comes to developing new products, assumption reversal can also stimulate creative ideas. Suppose you are developing a new ice-cream range. Here is a taster of the kind of assumptions you are likely to make:

- Ice-cream is cold.
- It comes in sweet flavors.
- It is packaged in tubs.
- It is smooth-textured.

... and many more. This kind of assumption reversal exercise could lead you to develop an ice-cream which comes in small lumps, perhaps in different favors, like jelly beans. Or you might come up with something which looks and tastes like ice-cream but isn't cold. Or maybe you could develop a range of savory ice-creams – tomato or avocado or sweet pepper. How about packaging ice cream in tins or tubes or jars or producing it in perforated sheets? Assumption reversal is a great way of generating these kind of wacky solutions.

Freeform assumption reversal

This is a variation on the basic technique, and is aimed at generating a creative atmosphere. It is a form of assumption reversal which isn't linked to a particular situation, but simply helps you to relax and come up with creative ideas. Just identify everyday assumptions or accepted situations and then smash them ... and see what happens. You can pick any assumptions you like, but here are a few examples to try:

- Suppose the only means of getting to work – for everyone – was by horse.
- Imagine that the cycle of night and day lasted a year instead of a day, so it was night for six months and then day for six months (if you live at the pole, don't bother with this one).
- What would happen if all workers were equal, with no bosses?
- Imagine if you had to keep on going to school until you were 40.

Let's take the first one as an example to see what sort of ideas it sparks off. For a start, everyone would have to own a horse, and stabling, and would have to find time to look after it. Everyone would have to work within a few miles of home. Offices and places of work would need stables instead of car parks. There would be a huge demand for silage and hay. People would become ambitious for a better cart or a top of the range carriage ... and so on.

This kind of exercise is useful as a starter to a creative session – solo or group – to put you in a creative frame of mind in which you are open to all sorts of quirky thoughts and ideas.

W hat are the attributes of a toothbrush? It's plastic; it has bristles at one end to clean teeth; it has a long thin handle to hold it by. Attribute listing is a fairly simple technique which involves identifying the key elements of a problem or product and then examining each in turn, looking for ways to improve it. So in the case of the toothbrush you might consider:

- making it out of a different material;
- using something other than bristles; or
- changing the shape of the handle.

The purpose of attribute listing is to get you to focus on aspects of a product or problem that you might otherwise overlook. You might

---

Individual technique: problem solving/idea generation

Professor Robert Platt Crawford developed this approach, in which you break down a problem or object into its component parts, or attributes, and analyze each in turn.

See also: Lotus blossom technique, Mind mapping, Morphological analysis.

normally consider ways to improve your range of toothbrushes by thinking in terms of the function of a toothbrush as a whole, but attribute listing helps you to consider individual aspects of it in isolation, such as the bristles.

This is attribute listing at its simplest, but you can list attributes for any problem or object. For a more complicated object, such as a personal organizer for example, you would need to list its features first and then the attributes of each feature. The adjoining table shows how your list might look.

Feature	Attributes
Closure	Popper
Cover	Leather
	Black
	Inside pockets
Binder	Metal ring clips
	6 clips
Dividers	A–Z/Jan–Dec
	Grey
	17 cm × 9.5 cm
Paper	White
	17 cm × 9.5 cm

Now you need to look at each attribute in turn and develop new ideas for improving it. Is there some other closure you could use than a popper? Could you expand on the idea of inside pockets? Do you have to use dividers and paper in the same size?

Physical attributes are not the only ones you can list. You can look at your subject from all sorts of angles. For example, you can list:

- *social attributes* – responsibilities, taboos, politics, leadership;
- *process attributes* – selling, marketing, manufacturing, distributing, time;
- *psychological attributes* – needs, motivation, image; and

- *price attributes* – cost to the supplier, manufacturer, wholesaler, retailer, customer.

Attribute listing is useful because it throws your focus onto features which you wouldn't necessarily consider otherwise. We tend to look at objects as a single unit, and describe them in terms of their function. If you manufactured personal organizers, for example, and were asked to describe one, you would probably explain that it was a single folder in which you could keep all your most important personal paperwork, especially your diary and address book, along with notes, accounts, street maps and so on.

You probably wouldn't detail every attribute – the fastening, the color of the dividers and so on. And this is why it's so easy to overlook these attributes when you are trying to solve problems or generate ideas. But it is often just these features which can stimulate the ideas you need.

One screwdriver manufacturer focused on the handle of its screwdrivers. This led them to the realization that most craftsmen and women use both hands to turn a screwdriver – at least sometimes – but that the handle only has room for one hand to hold it comfortably. So they redesigned the screwdriver with a handle suitable for using with both hands, and called it the Bacho Ergo screwdriver. Since then, Ergo tools have won huge acclaim for their design.

Example

Attribute listing is particularly useful for improving complicated products and service procedures. You can list the stages in a service process to solve a particular problem with quality, speed or cost: for each attribute come up with ideas related to improving quality or speed, or reducing costs. The adjoining table, using the physical attributes of the personal organizer, provides an example of a completed attribute list.

Feature	Attributes	Ideas
Closure	Popper	Ties, buckle, velcro
Cover	Leather	Plastic, board
	Black	Primary colors, patterns
	Inside pockets	Outside pocket for mobile phone
Binder	Metal ring clips	Lever arch
	6 clips	3 clips
Dividers	A–Z in 13 pairs	A–Z in 26 single sections
	Jan–Dec	18 month diary
	Grey	Primary colors, color code months
	17 cm × 9.5 cm	Taller with section markers at top instead of side
Paper	White	Pastel shades
	17 cm × 9.5 cm	Diary at top and addresses at bottom

Combined techniques

Attribute listing works well in conjunction with certain other techniques, especially for generating new ideas. For example you can use it to focus on a particular aspect of a product or service before going into a brainstorming session.

Another useful angle is attribute association chains. In this case you start as usual by listing features and attributes but you then take each attribute in turn and use *free association* (see p. 21) to generate a list of words as a basis for stimulating fresh ideas. The aim in the example given here is to cut the cost of manufacturing shampoo. First, list the features and their attributes.

Features	Attributes
Bottle	Plastic
	Clear
	Round
Lid	Plastic
	Grey
Label	Square
	Contains information
Shampoo	Viscous
	Mauve
	Cleans hair

Now, for each attribute, free associate four or five words. Here we take *shampoo* as an example.

Attribute	Free association
Viscous	Sticky – glue – paper – sheet – bed
Mauve	Purple – velvet – soft – tactile
Cleans hair	Scrubs – prison – cage – bars – alcohol

Then take each of these freely generated words and consider them in association with the attribute in question, to see if they inspire you to new ideas. Try to come up with an idea for each word, however hard it seems. You'll be surprised how quickly you get into it. Let's take the free association words for *viscous* as an example, and let's see what ideas they generate for a new approach to shampoo.

Free association	New idea
Sticky	Develop a shampoo that is tackier than others so it doesn't run through your fingers when you try to use it
Glue	Create a solid shampoo stick with special formulation shampoo to apply before washing to one part of the hair which is stuck together with food, bubble gum or whatever
Paper	Impregnate paper with shampoo so it can be rubbed on to wet hair. Can't spill or leak in transit
Sheet	Make a special pillowcase cover to use if you go to bed with damp hair. It speeds up the drying process as well as protecting the sheets
Bed	"Bed of roses" shampoo range scented by real preserved flowers or petals in the bottom of the bottle

Attribute analogy chains operate on a similar principle except that instead of using free association you use *analogies and metaphors* (see p. 16) to generate ideas. So the attribute *black* might generate the analogy *like being in a cave at night*; the attribute *January to December* might generate *a long year*. These analogies and metaphors give you a different angle for sparking off creative ideas.

Brainstorming

W hen you need quick answers to a fairly simple question, brainstorming is one of the most popular and most effective techniques. The word brainstorming is often used simply to mean getting together to come up with ideas, but true brainstorming is a much more specific thing.

It was developed in 1941 by Alex Osborn, a partner in an ad agency, to improve advertising ideas in both quantity and quality. Basically, members of the group offer ideas as they think of them – and they can be as wacky and offbeat as they like – and the ideas are written on a flipchart or board. The aim is to produce loads of ideas; quality is not important at this stage. The group reconvenes later to evaluate the ideas.

Group technique: idea generation

This is an anything-goes type of meeting which encourages a free flow of ideas in an atmosphere which is positive and aimed at consensus.

See also: Brainwriting, Lotus blossom technique, Mind mapping, Storyboarding, Synectics.

The principle is that you need to produce a high quantity of ideas in order to produce a high quality of ideas. The more ideas the group generates, the more of them will be really good; so you need to make it as easy as possible to volunteer ideas. In a good brainstorming session, the ideas will be falling over each other to come out much of the time.

The point about brainstorming is that you are not allowed to make any judgements on the ideas put forward. All too often, creativity is quashed by someone making an instinctive and negative assessment of a suggestion. How often, in meetings, do you hear:

- "We tried that before and it didn't work."
- "We can't afford that."
- "We haven't got the resources."
- "Customers just wouldn't go for that."
- "It wouldn't work."

These are the kind of criticisms which are banned in brainstorming sessions. As a result, people are free to make imaginative suggestions without feeling intimidated or inhibited. Some of these ideas may well be impracticable or inadvisable, but only by allowing all the duff suggestions can you let through the ideas that might look duff at first but could eventually turn out to be just the answer you needed. So the weak ideas are just as important as the good ones because they create the environment which allows good ideas to emerge.

The rules of brainstorming

In order to brainstorm effectively, you must follow the rules developed by Osborn. You need a group of between six and 12 people, from any department or background that seems relevant. If you have fewer than six you don't tend to generate enough ideas. More than 12, however, can become too intimidating (which is counter-productive) and can produce too many ideas to cope with. You also need a group leader, whose role we'll look at more closely in a moment. And you need someone whose job it is to record all the ideas somewhere that can be seen by everybody.

Here are the key rules to follow:

- No criticisms or judgements should be made about any idea. This is the most important rule of all.
- All ideas are encouraged, no matter how bizarre.
- The group should aim to produce as many ideas as possible.
- You can combine ideas to create new ones, or refine or build on other people's ideas.

A brainstorming session should usually last about half an hour to forty minutes; beyond that the ideas can start to dry up. The focus should be on the ideas themselves and not on who volunteered them. This should follow through to the evaluation later, since the lack of criticism during the brainstorm is not going to encourage people to open up if they know that everyone is just waiting for the evaluation session to make them feel stupid.

The group leader

The leader organizes the session and notifies the group in advance. This agenda should include all the relevant, objective facts about the topic to be brainstormed. At the start of the session the leader should repeat these to remind everyone what they are brainstorming and why. Then they should write the focal question where everyone can see it throughout the session.

The focal question is the reason you're all in the room. It might be "how can we improve our delivery service?" Or it could be "what new product lines should we be developing?" Or maybe "how do we stop customers breaking expensive goods on the shop displays?"

Now the leader opens the session by asking for suggested answers to the focal question. Their job becomes that of a facilitator: encouraging ideas, keeping the group focused on the question, and ensuring the rules are followed – especially the rule banning criticism.

Occasionally ideas can begin to flag during the session, in which case it is the leader's job to stimulate the flow. This can often be done simply by asking "what else?" or "any more ideas?" But sometimes specific techniques are needed to spark of a new chain of ideas, especially if some of the group are not naturally very creative thinkers. For example:

- Ask specific group members to come up with ideas.
- Give everyone in turn 30 seconds to come up with an idea.
- Use humor to relax people into a more creative frame of mind.
- Make one or two wacky suggestions to spark the group off.
- Ask abstract questions such as "what do people hate?" or "how do people like to be treated?" and get the group to relate the answers to the focal question to spark off fresh ideas.
- Introduce another technique such as *free association* (see p. 21), analogy (see p. 16) or forced relationship (see p. 86) briefly and use it to stimulate a new wave of ideas.

The evaluation session

You can't evaluate ideas during the brainstorming session or you will defeat the object of it. People cannot open up to free flowing ideas at the same time as closing off unusable ideas and crossing off options. Either you are broadening your horizons or you are narrowing them down. So the evaluation session has to take place later.

You can use the same leader to evaluate or choose a different group leader. Ideas should be sorted into related groups, and the group should rank the ideas according to usefulness and priority. The leader will need to encourage the group to consider all ideas, however wacky, rather than write them off on an instinctive judgement.

Although some judgement is inherent in evaluation, the leader still needs to encourage a positive approach, and make sure no one is made to feel stupid or embarrassed about an idea that was theirs. If the group likes an idea but thinks it is too expensive or impracticable, the leader should try to get the group to find a way round the problems, rather than give up. If the leader wants to motivate the group by reward, it is important to reward the group as a whole, or its members for participating, rather than to reward individuals for their ideas. This keeps the focus on the ideas and not on who generated them.

How to use brainstorming

Brainstorming works for answering relatively simple, specific questions. It is not designed to help you figure out complex technical problems or broad issues. You should only address one focal question in a session, and the session will probably burn out after half an hour or so. Up to this time, however, the leader should work hard to keep the ideas flowing.

Brainstorming's apparent simplicity leads some people to write it off on the basis that nothing that easy can be that much better than any old meeting to discuss a challenge or problem. Such people, however, are making a mistake. Brainstorming has been researched thoroughly, and the evidence is that it generates far more ideas than normal group meetings to address the same kind of questions. Its key features are its spontaneity, its positive approach to all ideas and its deferral of judgement. So long as these rules are adhered to, it is a highly effective approach, as thousands of organizations can attest.

Brainstorming variations

Visual brainstorming

Here's an interesting variation on brainstorming, which suits some people very well. Many people are visual rather than verbal thinkers, so instead of writing down ideas, get people to draw them. Other people may well be stimulated by drawings into coming up with fresh ideas of their own.

Another type of visual brainstorming involves getting group members to draw the problem or challenge:

1. List the attributes of the focal topic (see *attribute listing*, p. 31). For example, for ideas to improve the design of a piece of machinery, list each component part of the machine.
2. Next, get each person to choose one of these components and draw it in as much detail as they can.
3. Now lay all the drawings out, or pin them to the wall, so everyone can see them. Try to place the components in their approximate positions relative to each other.
4. Finally, get everyone to examine the drawings and use them as a springboard to launch new ideas from.

Take five

Take five is a variation on brainstorming which works with larger groups than 12, and can work well in groups with several members who are inhibited about volunteering ideas. It starts in the same way as a standard brainstorming session, with a focal question and a reminder of the facts and issues around it. After this:

1. Each participant spends the next two minutes compiling a list of ideas to help answer the question.
2. Participants then divide into groups of five and pool their ideas within the group.
3. Each group collectively ranks these ideas in order of importance.
4. The groups convene and create a short list of no more than ten ideas, made up of the most important ideas from each group.
5. This shortlist is then evaluated and discussed by all the participants together.

Solo brainstorming

There is a perfectly valid argument that you can't brainstorm alone. However, there is no reason why you shouldn't take as many of the best bits of brainstorming as possible and use them solo; after all, anything goes.

If you're brainstorming on your own, write down every idea you think of, without considering whether it is good or bad. Jot each one down on a separate slip of paper to make them easier to evaluate later. Once you have run out of ideas, sort the slips into related groups, and then rank the ideas in each group.

Examples

There are plenty of examples of improvements made by companies as a result of brainstorming sessions. Honda engineers came up with an idea at a brainstorming session which led to an increase in fuel efficiency of 35 percent in the Honda Civic VX.

One company used a brainstorming bulletin board, where a question was posted and everyone invited to pin ideas on the board around it. (These ideas in turn generate others, and the bulletin board can stay up for as long as you like.) The company announced on the board that it would pay $100 to any employee who produced an idea that saved the company money straight away. The first person to win posted a suggestion that the reward be cut to $50.

International Paper Company (IP) has opened a centre in New York to help customers design better packaging for their products. They bring together customers, their own packaging designers, scientists and technicians for brainstorming sessions. These sessions have produced several important and innovative new designs for packaging, such as a liquids container with a flat top which is more efficient to ship.

Brainwriting

B rainwriting is a silent version of brainstorming. But simply taking the noise and verbal interaction out of brainstorming changes the whole thing. In particular, it removes the possibility of the group leader favoring any particular participants; it can be hard to avoid giving priority to the ones who push their suggestions forward most vocally. Brainwriting can therefore be very useful if you have a mixed group where some people are much quieter than others, and you're concerned their ideas may go unvoiced or unheard. With brainwriting, everyone can come up with ideas simultaneously.

Brainwriting also puts the emphasis, more strongly than brainstorming does, on piggybacking on each other's ideas. Almost all the variations on it are based around this principle.

Group technique: idea generation

Brainwriting is similar to a written version of brainstorming, but with a strong emphasis on building on each other's ideas. It lacks a little in spontaneity, but gives everyone an equal input (brainstorming can favor whoever can shout the loudest).

See also: Brainstorming, Nominal Group Technique.

So what exactly is it? The basic brainwriting technique, developed at the Batelle Institute in Frankfurt, Germany, follows these steps:

1. The focal question is identified, so everyone knows what their ideas need to address.
2. Everyone sits around a table (about six to eight is the ideal group size), and each participant writes down their ideas for about five minutes – as many ideas as they can think of.
3. After five minutes, each person passes their sheet of paper to the person sitting next to them. For the next five minutes each person builds on the ideas they have been passed to add more ideas of their own.
4. After five more minutes the papers are passed on again, and the process continues. Three passes is generally enough, but you can continue if you think it will generate more useful ideas.
5. The leader collects up the papers and reads out the ideas. They can also be written up on a board. The group now evaluates the ideas it has generated (this can be deferred to a later session).

The same guidelines apply to brainwriting as to brainstorming:

- Encourage wild and wacky ideas.
- Don't allow criticism of anyone's suggestions.
- Defer judgement on all ideas until the evaluation at the end of the session.

As with brainstorming, this technique enables you to generate a very large number of ideas, including a large number of high quality ideas, in a very short time.

It can be harder to encourage bizarre ideas when people are not interacting as they are in verbal brainstorming, but it is often the craziest ideas which lead to the most creative answers. So if you have a group which needs help to come up with really offbeat ideas, here are a couple of techniques for teasing them out:

- Offer a reward for the most bizarre idea produced during the session.
- Explain that in the evaluation session you will take the two wackiest ideas and work on ways to make them practicable.
- One technique, known as the Brainwriting Game, involves competing to produce the craziest idea. Everyone writes down their craziest idea on a card, and the cards are then displayed. For the next 15 or 20 minutes, everyone goes round in silence and writes below everyone else's ideas suggestions to make them practicable – this will reduce their chances of winning the wackiest idea competition. At the end of this process, everyone votes on the most implausible idea. You also have a set of cards to evaluate which list bizarre ideas and ways to make them work.

Brainwriting variations

Brainwriting pool

A brainwriting pool works in a very similar way to the standard technique. Everyone writes down at least four ideas, and then puts their list in the middle of the table. Whenever anyone feels their ideas drying up, they simply swap their paper for one of the ones in the middle and carry on, piggybacking on the ideas on the new list.

The brainwriting pool can go on for about 25 to 30 minutes, and everyone should swap their list for one from the middle at least once. The big advantage of this system is that if the ideas are still flowing freely, no one has to pass on their sheet of paper. Everyone is free to get all their own ideas down first.

Method 6-3-5

Method 6-3-5 is a more structured approach to brainwriting. You need a group of six people sitting around a table. Each one draws three columns on a sheet of paper, and writes an idea relevant to the focal question at the top of each one. After five minutes they pass on the sheet to the next person. (6-3-5 derives its name from using six people with three ideas in five minutes.) Everyone now adds three more ideas which build on the ones they have been passed. The paper is passed on again to a total of six times – in other words until the papers have all been right the way round the group.

If your math is good you'll have realized that this method will generate 108 ideas in half an hour. Even allowing for duplications this is still a very high quantity of ideas to come up with.

Brainwriting versus brainstorming

Because of its similarity to brainstorming, brainwriting is often compared with it. Research indicates that brainwriting will generate more good ideas in the same length of time than brainstorming will. But most people find the atmosphere of a brainstorming session extremely stimulating, and can miss this during brainwriting if they compare the two approaches. If you find this is a problem, you can combine the two. Start by brainstorming the first few ideas to write down, and then use these as the basis for a brainwriting session.

Example

Imagine you are a printing company running a brainwriting session to come up with ideas for promoting your new range of stationery papers. Remember that ideas don't have to be limited by being practicable. A good idea can be made to work later. Just get the core idea down on paper. One of your half dozen finished brainwriting sheets might look like the list overleaf.

- Write to prospective customers on our new stationery range.
- Send top customers 100 compliment slips printed in their own logo, name and address on the new paper.
- Advertise a competition for the best company logo design; the winning company gets a free order of stationery on the new paper range.
- Hold a "guess how many sheets of paper in the bundle" competition at trade fairs.
- Send customers our own business card printed on the new range.
- Print top customers' logos in a range of colors on new paper/ or in black on a range of paper colors, and ask them to consider which they prefer.
- Send out an "invoice" on the new paper asking for competition entries instead of for money.
- Offer to take back old stocks of stationery in part exchange for orders for new stationery.
- Offer customers 100 free compliment slips or letterheads for their home address with every business order they place.
- Send out swatch books with the customer's own logo on each swatch.
- Send customers two duplicate sales letters in the same envelope, one on their usual paper and one on the new paper.
- Run a "spot the difference" competition at trade fairs to see if customers can rank different quality papers in order.
- Print on all invoices how much the order *would have* cost using the new paper.
- Glue the edges of letterheads and comp slips printed on the new range so they are supplied in tear-off pads – much neater and easier for storage.

Conscious Intuitive Techniques

"The supreme task ... is to arrive at those universal elementary laws from which the cosmos can be built up by pure deduction. There is no logical path to these laws – only intuition resting on sympathetic understanding."

Albert Einstein

W ell, if it was good enough for Einstein, it's good enough for us. The principle behind all these techniques is that the answer to your problem is somewhere inside your head, and you just have to find it. You know that feeling when a particular word or name is on the tip of your tongue, but you can't quite capture it: these techniques are conscious exercises to help your mind grasp the answer as it floats around in mental cyberspace.

Individual technique: problem solving

This is a bundle of techniques all of which are designed to steer your mind towards that sudden light-bulb moment when inspiration comes to you in a flash.

See also: Unconscious intuitive techniques.

As you may have realized, these techniques all assume that the answer is there to be found. In order for them to work, you need to accept this. If you think that you don't have the answer, it isn't logical to use this approach. You must believe that if your mind can simply make the right connection, you will solve your problem.

If you are grappling with a difficult problem, you often have the feeling that the answer is there but you can't quite reach it. Those are the times when it's worth using one of these techniques. The more complex a problem is, the more useful this kind of approach is. Complex problems require you to find connections between so many variables, that a flash of inspiration is often the only way to see the answer. Research increasingly shows that for the knottiest questions intuition often succeeds where rational thinking fails.

General guidelines

To use any of these techniques, you must first immerse yourself in the problem. Get to know it well, so that your mind is aware of all the factors that need taking on board. Then relax. Sometimes relaxation alone helps (see *Unconscious intuitive techniques*, p. 176), but all these techniques work better when you are relaxed. Turn down the lights, take a warm bath, have a glass of wine, take a catnap ... whatever helps you to wind down before you begin.

Then choose a technique you feel will work for you. If you're new to this, just pick one you like the sound of and try it. Most people have favorite techniques which they feel work best for them, although conventional wisdom would advise you to have as many different techniques as possible in your repertoire. Otherwise you can get stuck in a rut of always using the same approach, and being stuck in a rut is of course a block to creativity.

Visualization

There are different ways of using visualization to solve problems creatively. But the point is always to put you in the right frame of mind for finding the solution you need. They should all be relaxing, but they are more than simple relaxation techniques, because you make a conscious choice to visualize in a way which suits your problem.

Color visualization

This entails meditating on a particular color for about 15 minutes. After this, you speak or write affirmations of the color. Then let your mind go back to the problem and you often find that a solution jumps out at you.

We'll look at the detailed process in a moment, but the first thing to do is to choose a color which suits the problem and the kind of solution you want to find:

- *Red* is stimulating and exciting. Choose it for strength and stamina in attacking a problem.
- *Orange* is a warm, happy, touchy-feely color. It's a good one to use if you want to appeal to people (perhaps your problem involves attracting customers, or getting colleagues behind you).
- *Yellow* is inspirational. It's the color to choose when you want to increase your intuitive powers to find a solution that will involve making connections between different aspects of your problem.
- *Green* is the color of healing and harmony. It will increase your empathy and feeling for others (maybe you have an industrial relations problem to solve).
- *Blue* is the most relaxing color, although not the most creative. Choose it when you feel that tension and stress are getting in the way of finding a solution.
- *Indigo* is original and creative. It's the best color to choose if you're looking for highly creative approaches to a problem.
- *Violet* is creative too, in a more offbeat way. If you want your ideas to be not only creative but also radical – even revolutionary – choose violet.

So now you've chosen your color, what do you do with it? Set aside about 15 minutes or so and lie down somewhere comfortable with your eyes closed. Breathe deeply until you feel relaxed. You are ready to begin.

1. Say to yourself "I want the qualities of indigo" (or whatever color you have chosen).
2. Visualize a ball of indigo light above your head. See it touch your head and fill it with indigo, washing around and clearing your head of any negative thoughts or blocks.
3. Now let the light spread to your neck, massaging and cleansing it. Slowly allow it to spread down through your body, visualizing it clearly as it massages you and clears away any residual negative thoughts. See it spread to your shoulders, arms, hands and fingers. Let it fill your chest, lungs, heart, stomach, spine.
4. The indigo light should now flood down through your body and legs in a constant stream, from the top of your head to your toes, and then flow away from you. You are being continually bathed in indigo, clearing out any last vestige of resistance to creative indigo thoughts.
5. After a few minutes, open your eyes, trying to retain the sense that you are filled with indigo. Sit up slowly.
6. Finally, affirm – either aloud or writing on a pad – that you are indigo. You can choose your own affirmations but they should be something like: "I am indigo," "I have the creative qualities of indigo," "I am creative" and other positive statements. Believe them as you say or write them.

You should now find yourself feeling very different, and therefore able to look at your problem from an entirely different – and well selected – viewpoint. Amazing results can be achieved with this kind of intuitive approach.

A variation on color visualization involves choosing the appropriate color for your problem and then spending a day noticing anything you see in that color. If you also focus on your problem off and on throughout the day, your mind should begin to make links between the colored things you see and the problem. If you want to improve staff loyalty and you focus on green, you may (almost certainly) see a green tree sometime during the day. This might lead your mind to think of planting trees in the company grounds, and giving each employee their own spot and letting them choose and plant their own tree. That would give them a permanent link with the company.

Visualizing the problem

This is a very different approach from visualization. In this case you need to relax, close your eyes and visualize the problem. Maybe you need to find a more efficient system for repairing customers' products; perhaps your customers are spread all round the country but need a service engineer from your base within hours if the product breaks down.

Visualize the scenario. See the product break down, the customer identify the problem and call your engineers. See your engineers preparing to visit, and then go through the whole process of the journey, the arrival with the customer, and the repair. Go through it in as much detail as possible.

Often, a solution to your problem comes out of this process intuitively. It is more productive than physically going through the process, or examining the product, because your brain is not occupied with actually doing the thing; you can relax and put your full focus into the visualization.

Visualizing objects

This technique involves finding an object that relates to your problem in some way. For a financial or cost problem you might choose a ten dollar bill. For a security problem you might opt for a set of keys. If you want to improve morale, choose a book that makes you smile, or a poem that inspires you.

Physically hold the object you have chosen, and meditate on it for several minutes. Think about how it feels and smells, the sound it makes, and note these down on a sheet of paper. Move it around in your hands. Think about what it symbolizes, how it makes you feel, what memories it holds for you. Write down how you feel about it. Ask yourself what it can do for you, and write down the answers.

Choose a quality which the object represents for you. The quality of a set of keys might be *privacy*. Focus on this quality as you close your eyes. Imagine yourself being imbued with this quality as you hold the object. Do this until you feel full of the quality you have chosen, and then focus on your problem directing this quality at it.

Imagery

The idea behind this is that you can set your mind a challenge and then use an imagery technique to conjure up strong images. Note these images, and then look for links with your original challenge – the problem you are wrestling with. This is a powerful process and often throws up impressive results.

1. Start, as usual, by relaxing. Lie down somewhere comfortable and close your eyes.
2. Concentrate on the problem you want to solve. Form it into a question and ask your subconscious. For example: "How can I increase my employees' loyalty to the company?"
3. Now imagine you are going on a journey. You can buy tapes of guided meditations, or you might like to devise your own. For example: *You are walking down a sandy path between dunes onto a beach. You take your shoes off and feel the sand between your toes as you walk. You pass the tideline, full of seaweed and shells, pieces of driftwood and a crab claw. You continue down to the edge of the water and wait for the waves to wash over your feet. The first wave to come up is colder than you expected, and washes over your feet. Out to sea, you can see a huge tanker, but the rest of the sea and the beach is deserted. You turn right and walk along the water line … Your*

journey should last about 20 minutes, and should be as detailed as the example just given. Allow scope for a variety of images; you might take a boat trip, explore a cave, or turn inland and walk through a wood.

4. The journey might be anywhere – on a train, through a thunderstorm, in outer space – but at the end it is a useful technique to find a message concealed somewhere. It might be a piece of parchment in a treasure chest, a message in a bottle, a note in an envelope left on the mantelpiece of an empty house. Open it and see what it says.

5. Now concentrate on the images you have seen and open your eyes. Immediately write down or draw the images before you lose them. These are not only visual images, but also feelings, impressions, smells and any others. For example, you might record such things as warmth, seaweed, waves, cold and so on.

6. Use these images you have written or drawn to help you find the answer to your problem. Sometimes it will leap out at you; other times you will have to look long and hard to see the connections. The idea, however, is that your mind will throw up images which are relevant to the challenge you set it at the beginning.

Hypnogogic imagery

You produce hypnogogic images as you are drifting off to sleep, and it is these which this technique aims to tap into. As before, relax, close your eyes and focus on the challenge you are setting your mind. Try to empty your mind so that you begin to float off into sleep. Allow the sounds and images to appear.

Just before you lose control, wake up and record the sounds, shapes and images as quickly as possible, because they tend to recede very fast. Again, look for connections between these images and your problem.

If you are prone to fall asleep too quickly, there is a way round this. Salvador Dali used to use this technique to summon up images he could paint. He would relax in a chair holding a spoon. On the floor, beneath the spoon, was a metal plate. As he fell asleep the spoon would fall from his fingers on to the plate and wake him up.

Imaginary mentor

Small children often have imaginary friends, and many people retain these – or replace them with new imaginary friends – into adulthood. These imaginary friends can be not only companions but also mentors. General MacArthur used to call up his father for advice on his strategy in the Pacific. Mozart and Milton, both as creative as you could realistically aspire to be, had their own inner guides.

The gist is that if you are relaxed enough your unconscious mind – through your imaginary mentor – will be able to converse with you without being controlled by your conscious mind. This can throw up answers to problems that you wouldn't arrive at through conscious thought alone. In effect, this means that if you are relaxed enough you may control both halves of the conversation to begin with, but your mentor will begin to speak with a mind of their own.

Clearly you need to start by choosing a mentor. They can be real or imaginary, alive or dead. You can choose your grandfather, an ancient goddess, Fred Flintstone, Einstein ... whoever you feel personifies the aspect of your unconscious that you want to summon up. Perhaps you want someone with a more serious outlook than you, or a more wacky one, or more rational. Most people have just one mentor who personifies a quality which they regularly need to access. But you might have two or three you can call on. However, regularly using the same mentor works best for most people, rather than picking someone new each time. That way you can build up a solid relationship.

Once you have chosen your imaginary mentor, you are ready to converse with them:

1.   As with all these techniques, the first thing to do is to relax. Lie down and close your eyes.

2. Imagine a soft, glowing white light around you, bathing your body.
3. Now imagine yourself walking into a favorite place – a house, a beach, a wood, a garden. Imagine all the detail you can; the smell, the sounds, the atmosphere. Make it as real as you can.
4. Now see your mentor walking towards you. Study their face, and see what emotions you feel. Be as detailed as you can.
5. Now ask your mentor: "Please guide me. Help me to find a resolution to my problem." Explain the problem and give all the necessary facts. Be as natural and realistic as possible, and listen to your mentor's responses.
6. Have a conversation with your mentor, and take on board whatever they say just as you would with a real person sitting beside you in the room.
7. End the conversation and have your mentor invite you to call them up whenever you need to, and reassure you that they are there to help you.
8. Open your eyes, and record what your mentor has said to you.

Example

An importer was having trouble selling car seat covers made from wooden beads. They were very popular in Asia, but he couldn't overcome the resistance he encountered in the US because the concept was unfamiliar to people. He used a color visualization and focused on the color yellow. Suddenly the image of a yellow New York taxi came into his head.

He gave a free seat cover to taxicab drivers, and persuaded them to use it. The drivers liked it. Passengers asked about it and the taxi drivers made great salespeople – and the seat covers each had the importer's phone number displayed on the back. Sales now run at well over 100,000 seat covers a year.

Crawford Slip Method

T he Crawford Slip Method, or CSM, was developed in the US in the 1920s by CC Crawford. It is particularly useful for addressing complex problems, especially where you need input from a lot of people. You can use CSM with a group of hundreds, but it is most commonly used with groups of about 20 or 30. (Its name is derived from the fact that everyone writes suggestions and ideas on slips of paper.)

Broadly speaking, the group leader devises a detailed set of target statements, designed to elicit responses from the group. Participants are then given a pile of slips or small index cards each, and asked to write down ideas, using a fresh slip for each idea. All the ideas are then incorporated into a final report.

Group technique: problem solving

A large group spends a short time writing down as many ideas as possible in response to a detailed set of statements and questions. The ideas are each recorded on a separate slip of paper and then incorporated into a report.

See also: Rice storm.

CSM differs from many other creative techniques in several ways:

- It works best with large groups. Each person may generate around 20 ideas in a session, so a group of 25 people might give you 500 ideas.
- CSM is devised to cope with complex problems.
- It starts from a detailed set of statements about the problem, where the majority of techniques start from a single focal question.
- The participants are not generally involved in the process after submitting their ideas.
- The end product is a report which should incorporate all the ideas barring duplications. The leader alone, or a task force, compiles the report.

Target statements

The starting point for CSM is the target statements, which are compiled in advance. A target statement consists of a basic problem area, a stated overall problem, and additional statements which help define the problem. An example is shown in targets "A" and "B."

Target A: office move planning (basic problem area)

What are the key challenges of the move? (overall problem)

- What concerns employees most about the move?
- What are the main difficulties involved in planning the move?
- What are the main frustrations, problems, bottlenecks, delays of the move expected to be?
- Write each frustration, problem or difficulty related to the move on a separate slip.

Target B: logistics of the move (basic problem area)

How to make the move physically (overall problem)

- Solutions are just problems in reverse.
- What are your best suggestions for remedying the problems you just identified?
- What have you seen or heard of other people doing that worked well?
- If you were in charge, what would you change to make things run more smoothly?
- Write your first thoughts on a slip; don't wait for a better idea to come.
- Write each idea on a separate slip.

You might add more target statements, up to about three or four for a session. It all depends on what you want from the group. You might add a target statement relating to morale problems associated with the move, for example.

The key steps

1. Once the target statements are prepared, the group meets. Participants are each given a stack of slips or small index cards to write their ideas on. These should be deliberately small to keep the ideas concise, and to make the next stages easier.
2. The participants are given the first target statement and asked to write their ideas on the slips. Give them about ten minutes to do this. Then move on to the next statement.
3. At the end of the session collect the slips and thank the participants for their ideas.

4. Now perform the data reduction and write the report (we'll look at this in more detail in a moment).

The rules of engagement

There are certain rules which the participants in CSM should follow when writing their ideas on the slips. These are intended to make the ideas clear and concise, and easy to use for the later stages of the process.

- Write along the long side of the slip, not across the short end.
- Write on the top edge of the slip.
- Write one sentence only on each slip.
- If an idea requires an explanation, write the explanation on a separate slip.
- Use short sentences and simple words.
- Write in note form (don't bother with words like "it" or "which").
- Don't use jargon.
- Write out acronyms in full, at least the first time you use them.
- Keep writing until the leader calls time.

Compiling the report

Once the session is over, you have a huge pile of slips or index cards. The next stage is to sort these out. Begin by organizing them into lots of general categories, removing duplications as you go. Then combine these into a few major categories.

You should now be able to see an outline for your report, which you compile as you would any other report, incorporating the ideas on the slips into sections, paragraphs and bullet points.

As you can see, the end result of CSM is the kind of report most managers frequently prepare. The only difference is that in the space of half an hour or so, CSM gives you a huge reservoir of valuable ideas to draw on, and everyone you involve in the process shares in the ownership of the final report. As with many creative thinking techniques, the process is of great diplomatic importance, in making everyone feel they have had an input into the final solution, process or decision.

CSM in action

Imagine that you are in an increasingly competitive hi-tech industry, with a growing need for top quality, well trained, motivated staff in areas of the business where you have not previously invested heavily in personnel. You have agreed that the key to remaining competitive is to change your recruitment strategy, but you have not yet examined how to achieve this effectively.

This is a good opportunity to bring senior managers together for a creative session using CSM, beginning with your first target statement "A".

Give everyone about ten minutes to write all their ideas on slips of paper or small index cards, and then collect these in. Pin up the next target statement "B" (or hand round copies) and give the group another ten minutes or so to record ideas related to these statements and questions.

Target A: changing our employee profile

Employing top quality people

- A business is only as good as the people it employs.
- What will be the key benefits of employing the best people?
- What will be the implications in terms of cost, training, staff turnover, team relationships?
- What will be the effect from our customers' point of view?
- Write each idea on a separate slip.

Target B: suitable applicants

How can we locate suitable people?

- Where are the best people likely to be?
- How can we let them know that we want to hear from them?
- What are likely to be the biggest problems in identifying and attracting the attention of the best people?
- Write each idea on a separate slip.

Now repeat the process again with your final target statement "C":

Target C: attracting top people

How can we persuade people they would like to work for us?

- Recruitment is a two-way process.
- What factors will determine whether people want to come and work for us?
- What could we offer that other companies don't, which would have real appeal?
- How can we let potential applicants know that we are worth applying to?
- What do you consider the plus points of working for this particular company?
- What are the minus points of working for this company?
- Write each idea on a separate slip.

At the end of this process, collect up all the slips. You can now use these ideas to produce your report, which will cover:

- the benefits of changing your recruitment strategy;
- the effects of the new strategy;
- how to reach potential applicants;
- how to encourage applications from the right people; and
- how to make sure that the best people want to work for you.

Delphi Technique

I n ancient Greece, if you wanted to know the future, you asked the oracle at Delphi. The Delphi technique is quite specialized; you would only use it when you wanted to call on the ideas of a group of experts (who are probably geographically separated) to produce a forecast. It has been used, for example, to make predictions ranging from future trends in logistics management to expected tourism levels in Singapore.

The technique for this kind of forecasting is a little long-winded, but effective. You need to construct a questionnaire based around the scenario you want forecast. This questionnaire is then mailed (or e-mailed) to each of your experts.

Group technique: problem solving

This non-interactive forecasting technique generates creative input from a disparate group of people. Questionnaires are mailed to each member of the group, their responses combined and refined, and then returned to them. This process continues until consensus is reached.

See also: Nominal group technique.

When the results are returned, they must be analyzed and summarized. These summaries are then returned to the experts, who are asked to revise their responses where necessary. If any response varies widely from those of the rest of the group, the expert is asked to justify their difference of opinion.

The revised responses, and any justifications, are then summarized and circulated again. This process of summarizing and revising continues until the group reaches a consensus.

Pros and cons

This technique arguably generates a lower level of creativity than some; however it does have a number of advantages to offset this:

- It can bring together the ideas of experts who are geographically separate.
- Everyone has an equal input.
- Ideas remain linked to the person who generated them, which can be useful when experts are being used.
- Ideas are not influenced by pressure from the rest of the group.

There are disadvantages to the Delphi technique, which you need to take into account before you use it:

- The quality of the questionnaires and the input of the analyst are hugely important in the success of the process.
- It is time-consuming, even if you use e-mail to communicate with your group of experts. Summarizing and refining the responses takes time.
- It lacks the spontaneity of many other creative techniques.

Example

Suppose you want your group of experts to predict the most important trends over the next ten years in your industry – say it's the fast food industry. A typical set of questions is contained in the adjoining questionnaire.

Questionnaire

- What are the greatest threats facing the fast food industry over the next ten years?
- What are the greatest opportunities?
- What will fast food customers be looking for in terms of service?
- What will customers want in terms of product range?
- How do you see the size of the fast food market changing in the next ten years?

Take the first question as an example. You might find that you get a list of twenty threats. In that case, try to summarize them into broad categories – too much competition, increasing costs, lack of suitable locations – and return this summary to your experts for them to agree or revise. Perhaps just one of your experts came out of left field and suggested that a huge increase in vegetarianism would threaten the conventional fast food market. In that case ask them to justify this prediction, and circulate their evidence.

Go through this process with the whole questionnaire. After a couple more trips back and forth, you should arrive at a summarized response to your questionnaire which all your experts are happy with.

Discontinuity

A n accountant I used to work with had an unusual way of solving problems. If he simply couldn't fathom out why, for example, the books didn't balance, he would say: "Time to change my socks." He would then remove his shoes, take off his socks and turn them inside out, put each one back on the other foot, and replace his shoes. Then he would straighten up, look at the ledger again, and say: "Aha. This is wrong here. The customer changed the order on Tuesday morning, I remember now, and we put through a credit note and we also cancelled the original order ..." It was uncanny how this apparently pointless sock-changing palaver gave him the solution almost every time.

In fact, this is a perfect example of discontinuity. Habitual behavior does not stimulate our thinking. But by putting ourselves into

---

Individual technique: problem solving/idea generation

The principle behind this is that your mind can get stuck in a rut, which inhibits creativity. Discontinuity is an approach which forces you out of the rut by introducing untypical behavior or ideas to jar you into a new way of thinking.

See also: Random stimulation.

a new mode of operating, we force our minds to see the world differently, which often leads us to new realizations and connections. The point about changing the socks was that it was a conscious act designed to make my colleague feel different. Feeling different is only a small step away from thinking differently.

As a creative technique, discontinuity is about forcing yourself to look at things from a fresh perspective by upsetting routines or by thinking in a way to which your mind is unaccustomed.

Creating discontinuity

Changing your socks is not your only option (good news for anyone who doesn't wear socks). There are two key types of discontinuity you can create: discontinuity of behavior and discontinuity of thought.

Discontinuous behavior is just a matter of doing things differently. Coming into work early, or taking the train instead of driving. You could watch a television program you don't normally watch, or read a children's book (if you are a parent, try reading a grown-up book for a change). Eat food you never generally eat, or buy yourself bright pink underwear. Hold your meetings in the park instead of the office, or stand on a chair to hold phone calls. Try talking in a different accent all day. Ask your colleagues to address you by a different name. Get tipsy at lunchtime – or if this is your usual style, try staying sober all afternoon.

Discontinuity is a fun technique, and you'll find you start to think differently. The only rule is that you can't keep repeating the same behavior change, or it ceases to be discontinuous. If you get your colleagues to address you as Myrtle every day, it will slip into habit within a few days.

Discontinuous thinking is about provoking our minds into new thought paths by thinking in a new way. This juxtaposes old and new thinking to produce creative ideas. The way to do this is to give your mind something untypical to think about. It may be a piece of poetry or an inspirational quote. But don't use your favorite poem which you know by heart; find something new – perhaps by opening an anthology at random.

Zen Buddhists use Zen koans to force their minds to open up and think creatively. A koan is a short story, usually about a Zen master and student, which is designed to reveal a great truth to those who can understand it. If you grew up in the 60s, you'll probably enjoy this approach to discontinuous thinking. Even if you didn't, you may well find it stimulating. Here is an example:

A Zen master wanted to appoint a monk to open a new monastery. He told his students that the job would go to whoever answered his question most ably. He placed a jar of water on the ground and said: "Who can say what this is without speaking its name?"

The chief monk said, "It can't be called a wooden shoe." The cooking monk, who was named Isan, tipped the jug over with his foot and left.

The Zen master smiled and said, "The chief monk has lost." So Isan became master of the new monastery.

You can think about your poem, quote or koan for a while and then go back to your problem and see if you look at it in a different light. Or, as a more general approach to creative thinking, start each day with a different koan or a new inspirational piece of writing.

Discontinuity is a driving force behind Edward de Bono's invented word, "Po," which stands for "provocative operation;" something which jerks you out of your existing pattern of thinking. It is also the principle underlying Roger von Oech's bestselling creativity book, *A Whack on the Side of the Head*.

Discontinuity in action

Suppose you're puzzling over how to handle promotions in your department. You have two very able people, but only one can be promoted to the newly vacated post. You would be happy to promote either, and don't want to set up rivalries and resentment. After worrying away at the problem for a while, you decide to try discontinuity to help you find a new angle on it.

The precise nature of the discontinuity isn't important since it doesn't need to relate to the problem in any way – it simply needs to jolt you into a new viewpoint. So you decide that tomorrow morning you will come into work by train instead of by car, and you'll read a Gary Larson cartoon book on the train (a good choice for discontinuous thinking). Instead of working in your own office, you'll share a desk with one of your team and work in the open plan office with everyone else. You'll have a lunchtime drink at the pub with some of your staff instead of working through. And you won't think about the problem again until you're on the train on the way home.

By the time you head home, you should be in a very different frame of mind from usual, and able to approach your problem from a different perspective. This can lead to new insights. For example, why not create two new posts of equal status and promote both your star people? Or devise some kind of job share so that they both share the function of the vacated post, with salary and job titles to reflect the new workload? By freeing yourself up to wander around the problem and look at it from new angles, discontinuity can give you some lateral solutions.

Drawing Techniques

Creativity is handled in the same (right) hemisphere of the brain as visual skills, while verbal skills are located in the left hemisphere. This means that many people find it easier to link creative and visual skills together than creative/verbal skills, since you focus your thinking in only one side of the brain. So if you try a pictorial approach to creative thinking you may find your creative juices flow more freely. This technique may work especially well for men, since they are typically more inclined to use one hemisphere of the brain at a time, while women's brains seem to use both sides at once more readily.

If you are already a keen doodler, you may well realize its benefits. If you aren't, these techniques will have the added benefit for

---

Individual/group techniques: idea generation

Many of us like to doodle while we're on the phone, or to sketch an object as we talk about it to get a clearer picture – literally. This group of techniques draws on the brain's ability to think visually as well as verbally.

See also: Brainwriting, Conscious intuitive techniques, Left-brain/right-brain thinking, Pattern language.

you of opening up a new way of thinking, which in itself is a spur to creativity.

Draw your problem

One of the simplest drawing techniques is simply to sit down with your pen and paper and draw your own perception of the problem. If you were designing a kitchen and you wanted to work out how to fit in all the appliances and the furniture, you would probably do this without thinking. But try it for less obviously visual problems.

Perhaps you are trying to solve the problem of customer complaints about frequent late deliveries. Try drawing out the delivery routes, or drawing the delivery vehicles, or even drawing an angry customer shouting at a driver. Simply by focusing the right side of your brain on the problem, you often spark off a solution.

Doodles and scribbles

If you want to take a more abstract approach, focus on your problem and then just doodle the first thing that comes into your mind, concrete or abstract. As with all creative and intuitive techniques, it helps to do this when you are already relaxed. Many people like to draw a border of some kind around the page, which represents the parameters of the problem or challenge so as to help you focus on it. You might also want to experiment with:

- drawing with your other hand;
- drawing with your eyes closed;
- drawing with colored pencils; or
- using ink splashes, sponged patterns and other methods of creating images.

You can keep drawing for as long as you feel you want to, and complete one drawing or several. When you have finished, study your drawing or doodle. Look at the whole picture and at individual parts of it. Somewhere in the drawing, you should see something which helps you to a realization about your problem or challenge. Look for patterns and shapes, or relevance in objects or people you've drawn.

Brainsketching

This is a very different technique, and a group one, but it also harnesses the creative power of visual thinking. It is very similar to brainwriting but uses visual images rather than words. Here's what you do:

1. After establishing the focal question, each member of the group draws an idea for a solution on a sheet of paper in front of them. This can be a clear illustration of the solution but it doesn't have to be. It can be abstract or symbolic. Group members should not talk while they are doing this.
2. After a set time – five minutes is about right – everyone passes their drawing on to the person next to them.
3. On receiving the new drawing, each group member studies it and then tries to improve it. This might entail adding to it, making notes on it, or perhaps drawing a fresh sketch inspired by it.
4. Repeat this process until time is up; three passes is generally enough.
5. The whole group now evaluates the ideas on each sheet of paper.

Examples

Thomas Edison was a keen visual thinker. Before he formulated an important idea, he used to make hundreds of sketches and abstract doodles. Many of his doodles which he drew before inventing the light bulb still exist, although they are meaningless to just about everyone else.

Another keen doodler was Leonardo da Vinci. He used to scribble randomly on a sheet of paper with his eyes closed. When he had finished, he studied the page for patterns, people, events or objects in the random lines. This, apparently, produced many of his best inventions and works of art. Da Vinci wrote:

"I must mention a new method of study which, although it may seem trivial and almost ludicrous, is very helpful in awakening the mind to all sorts of inventions. When you look at a stain-spotted wall you may recognize a similarity to various landscapes beautiful with mountains, rivers, boulders, trees. Or you might see battles and men in action, or strange faces and outfits, and an infinite variety of things which you could clarify into whole, well-drawn forms."

Excursion Technique

S uppose you have a really difficult problem to solve. You've already tried another technique, perhaps brainstorming, but the group hasn't come up with a solution. This is when the excursion technique is likely to prove useful. It works especially well if the problem is quite narrow in scope, and when you know you need a radical solution but you can't quite put your finger on it.

Maybe you are trying to find a way to design a motorized pushchair that doesn't present any safety hazards. So far every possible solution you've come up with presents another problem, but you're convinced there's an answer if only you could look at the problem in the right way.

The excursion technique has four basic steps. Here's an overview:

Group technique: problem solving

This technique pulls out all the stops to solve really knotty problems by combining visualization and analogy techniques in a group setting.

See also: Forced relationship, Synectics.

---

1. *The excursion itself* – each member of the group goes on a personal visualized journey and records what they see.
2. *Analogies* – each person now finds analogies between the images from the excursion and the problem at issue.
3. *Evaluating the analogies* – the next step is to identify the practical use of these analogies so as to create solutions to the problem.
4. *Sharing with the group*.

The excursion

The group leader reminds everyone of the problem they are there to solve. Then each person closes their eyes and spends about ten minutes going on a private visual journey of their own in a location given to them by the leader. If any members of the group are unused to this, it is very important that the leader coaches them in order to ensure that they let their imaginations run freely.

- The excursion can be to any place the leader determines, real or imaginary. You might choose a railway journey, a theme park, a farm, a mountain road, a World War I trench, a journey through space, a walk through a favorite city ... anywhere you like.
- The important thing is for participants to let their imaginations run. Anything goes; they can visualize whatever comes to them.
- They should examine everything on their excursion in detail. If they take a walk through a wood they should notice, for example, the leaves, the type of trees, whether it's sunny or overcast, the sound of the twigs cracking beneath their feet, any wildlife – squirrels, birds, wild flowers, toadstools – the smell of the place ... in other words everything they would notice if they were really there, looking around and taking it all in.

The participants should record what they see on the left hand side of a sheet of paper. So for the example above they might list oak trees, acorns, sunshine, crackling twigs, squirrel, toadstools, and so on. They can do this either as they go along or after they have finished. Many people prefer to make these notes at the end of the excursion otherwise they have to open their eyes during it, which can break their thread.

The analogies

The next step is for each participant to spend about 15 minutes looking for analogies between the objects on their list and the problem they are there to solve. So if you're trying to design a safe motorized pushchair, you might come up with something similar to the adjacent two-column table.

Observation	Analogy
Oak trees	Pushchair motor should be strong and long-lasting
Acorns	An acorn is smooth and rounded so that you can't hurt yourself on it
Sunshine	Sunshine gives strength and life to plants and animals, just as the motor does to the pushchair
Crackling twigs	The cracking sound of the twigs is like the noise of the motor.
Squirrel	Squirrels hide things, just as the motor should be hidden out of reach
Toadstools	Toadstools appear and disappear overnight, and the motor should come on and go off as it is needed

You don't have to be pedantic about using only analogies; what matters is to find some kind of relationship between the object visualized and the problem you want to solve.

Evaluation

This is really the most crucial stage. Each group member now has to decide how the analogy or relationship between each object and the problem can actually be used to find a solution. These are the ideas you are here to generate, and this is just as creative a process as the first two steps. The ideas generated should be written down in a third column appended to the existing two-column table.

Observation	Analogy	Solution
Oak trees	Pushchair motor should be strong and long-lasting	No batteries which can run down, no fuel which needs refilling
Acorns	An acorn is smooth and rounded so that you can't hurt yourself on it	Entire motor unit enclosed in a smooth sphere
Sunshine	Sunshine gives strength and life to plants and animals, just as the motor does to the pushchair	Solar power?
Crackling twigs	The cracking sound of the twigs is like the noise of the motor	Clockwork mechanism or dynamo
Squirrel	Squirrels hide things, just as the motor should be hidden out of reach	Enclose the motor and prop shaft inside a childproof casing between the front wheels which is disguised as a footrest
Toadstools	Toadstools appear and disappear overnight, and the motor should come on and go off as it is needed	Motor which winds up as you push along or downhill, and helps propel the pushchair uphill when you release it

Sharing

The final step is the one which introduces valuable group interaction. Each member of the group shares with the others the ideas on their list, starting with the excursion and the analogies, before going on to explain the solutions. The group as a whole can then build on these ideas to come up with a workable solution. In this example, you might end up designing a pushchair driven, when going uphill, by a dynamo concealed beneath the footrest, and recharged by the motion of pushing the pushchair on the flat or downhill. As you see, not every idea is incorporated – you might in fact have pursued the solar power route instead – and other participants may have generated very different but equally valid ideas. But the excursion technique has produced a solution to a long-standing problem.

Example

This is a very creative process which combines more than one technique. This is one reason why it is so effective. By the time group members begin to share their ideas they should be in a very creative mode. Consequently some of the ideas may be reached very indirectly... but hey! Who cares so long as you find the answers you need?

One instance of this is a group of people from NASA who wanted to find a way to fasten space suits. Since this was proving difficult, the group leader decided to try using the excursion technique. He got the group members to go on an imaginary journey through a jungle. In the final, sharing stage of the exercise, one man described being "clawed at by weeds" and, as he said this, he demonstrated by clasping his hands together with his fingers interlocked. Although this meant little to him, the other members of the group made comment on the gesture and discussed it. To them, it was reminiscent of Velcro clasping as it overlaps. The eventual solution to their problem was a kind of Velcro-style fastener.

FCB Grid

The FCB grid was the brainchild of Richard Vaughn of the Foote, Cone and Belding advertising corporation. He devised it to help identify the market position of products and services, and to spot any gaps in the market. If you want to analyze your position relative to that of your competitors, or to look for market gaps, or – like Richard Vaughn – formulate a marketing strategy, try drawing an FCB grid.

Start by drawing a four-cell matrix. On one axis mark *high involvement* and *low involvement*, and on the other mark *think* and *feel* (see Fig. 1, p. 82).

Individual technique: idea generation

The FCB grid is a simple matrix, which helps you identify and position new products and services by creating a visual representation of their place in the market.

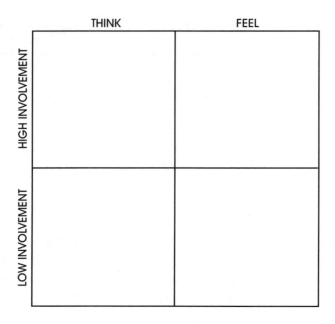

Fig. 1

- *High involvement* represents expensive products and services such as holidays, cars and computers.
- *Low involvement* represents inexpensive products and services such as dry cleaning, groceries or stationery.
- *Think* represents products and services with which customers are not emotionally involved, but choose on the basis of verbal, numerical, analytical, cognitive criteria. These are such things as computer software, cameras and dishwashers.
- *Feel* represents products or services that have an emotional appeal such as beauty products, clothes and fiction books.

You can now place any product in the correct quadrant of the matrix. For example, you would put breakfast cereal in the bottom left – *low involvement/think* – quadrant. A mortgage goes in the top left section. An expensive designer wedding dress belongs in the top right, and everyday make-up goes in the bottom right.

To make the FCB grid useful, however, you need to take this one step further. You also need to place products in the right part of the quadrant. So a life insurance policy would be part way up the high involvement square, but not as high up as a house or a luxury boat. On the other hand, it would be well over to the left of the *think* section, since it is selected by the customer on almost entirely functional rather than emotional criteria.

A sports car, on the other hand, is also a *high involvement* product, but is probably selected more on the basis of feeling than thinking. Concrete data about performance is important, so it should be close to the 'think' side, but it is generally the image of the car that sells it, so it goes in the top right cell (see Fig. 2).

You can place your own products in their rightful positions in the matrix, and you can also put your competitors' products in place. This way, you can see how a group of products is spread out around the matrix. You might find that your product falls in the middle of a cluster of competitors' products, or that it is located somewhere very

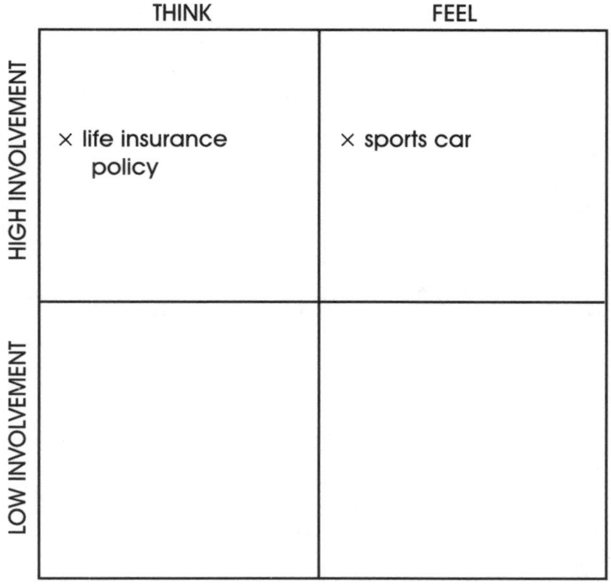

Fig. 2

different. Or you might establish that your own product or service range is grouped closely together, and you are missing opportunities to diversify.

The FCB matrix is a valuable way to generate ideas. You might notice that you have products everywhere except in the bottom right quadrant. This should spur you to look for mileage in developing *low involvement/feel* products.

You can, of course, put anything else you want to on your axes. You might have a range of fridges with varying capacity, and different sized ice-compartments. If you arrange these on an FCB grid (numbering each product in the range to make the grid easier to read), it might look something like the one shown in Fig. 3.

This makes it very easy to see at a glance that what you don't have is a low capacity fridge with a large ice compartment. Perhaps there is a market for this, with people who buy a lot of frozen foods.

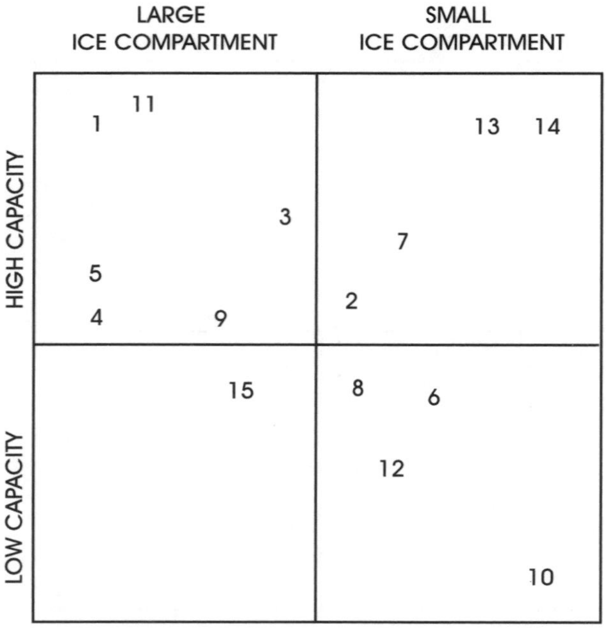

Fig. 3

Example

One of the very best advertisements for the FCB grid is Apple Computers. Before launching, Apple drew up a grid of the computer market. All the main players were selling computers in the *high involvement/think* quadrant. Going into the same type of market as these huge organizations such as IBM would have been lunacy. So Apple decided to position themselves diametrically opposite, in the *low involvement/feel* sector.

They made a computer for ordinary people instead of for experts, and they called it a personal computer – a much more *feely* name than, for instance, a minicomputer. They adopted a marketing strategy, which emphasized that their computers were part of a whole new concept, designed for non-experts and really user-friendly. And this was the strategy that made them so successful competing against the giants of the industry.

Forced Relationship

S ometimes the key to finding new ideas lies in combining existing ideas or concepts. Forced relationship techniques work by making you find connections that you might not otherwise have seen. There are various ways of doing this, some of them reminiscent of other techniques. Two of the key ones are the circle of opportunity, and forced analogy.

Circle of opportunity

This technique starts with a list of twelve key attributes of the product or service you are trying to generate ideas around (see *Attribute*

Individual technique: idea generation

The spur to creativity in this technique comes from forcing your mind to make connections between two apparently unconnected things, one of which relates to the ideas you want to generate.

See also: Analogies and metaphorical thinking, Morphological analysis, Random stimulation, Two words technique.

listing, p. 31). Imagine you are a tour operator trying to develop a new type of holiday. You would list attributes such as destination, food, transport, warm, distance, sunshine, luxury, swimming, activity, accommodation, time, children. You are looking for twelve words, which you associate with holidays; but it doesn't matter which twelve you choose.

1. Draw a circle and mark off twelve numbered points around it, like a clockface. Beside each of these numbers, write a key attribute (see Fig. 4).
2. Now throw two dice to choose an attribute. Then throw a single die to choose another attribute.
3. Think about both these attributes separately and in combination. Think of unusual ways to develop these attributes, and ways of combining both attributes. For example, you might have thrown 4 and 11: distance and children. How can you combine these? Perhaps you could run holidays where the children stay

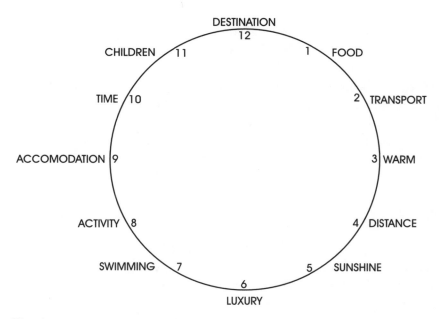

Fig. 4

separately from their parents – near enough to keep an eye but far enough for a bit of peace and privacy. Or maybe you could organize long distance holidays for children without their parents but with qualified adults to look after them.

4. Free associate the two attributes, separately and together. For example, distance might give you: *space, emptiness, room, door.* Children might give you: *playing, swing, fresh air, weather.* Now use these words to help you find other ideas. For example, *space* and *weather* might make you think of wide open spaces where you can watch the weather – maybe holidays to view solar eclipses or chase twisters. *Door* and *playing* might give you the idea of an indoor play area for kids – perhaps self-catering chalets which include a child's playroom equipped with toy cars, indoor slides and other toys.

5. You can also use these attributes as the basis for other techniques such as mindmapping or brainstorming. Although circle of opportunity is generally used as an individual technique, it can also work well in a group session.

As a variation of this technique, you might choose general attributes, rather than ones that relate to your particular topic. For example, you might list the items shown in Fig. 5.

This is a circle of opportunity, which you might use time and again to generate different product ideas. Or you might list functional attributes of a process, such as selling, marketing, promotion, manufacturing, time, economy and so on. It's up to you to decide which attributes will help you find the ideas you're looking for.

Forced analogy

In the analogy technique on p. 16, the aim of the exercise was to find an analogy for your problem. Forced analogy, however, doesn't allow you such a luxury. You can't choose the analogy. This is much better suited to finding new ideas than to solving problems, although it can be used for either.

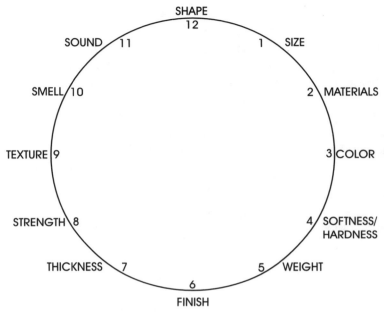

Fig. 5

The gist is simple. You simply compare the subject you want ideas for with something else that has nothing obvious in common with it. Then you have to find similarities between the two. You can generate random objects to compare your subject with in several ways:

- Open a book at random and find a word.
- Prepare a list of about 60 words and write each one on a card. Then choose a card at random.
- Cut pictures out of magazines, stick them on cards and use these instead of words.

Now list the attributes of this randomly chosen object, and then find a similarity with your subject for each one. So for your holiday ideas, you might find the word *tree*. List the attributes of a tree first of all, and then find analogies between these and a holiday. Use these analogies to generate ideas.

Example

In his book *The Art of Creative Thinking*, Robert Olson shows how to draw analogies about a corporate organization structure from a matchbox.

Attributes of a matchbox	Corporation
Striking surface on two sides	The protection an organization needs against strikes
Six sides	Six essential organizational divisions
Sliding center section	The heart of the organization should be slideable or flexible
Made of cardboard	Inexpensive method of structure – disposable

Force-field Analysis

Kurt Lewin originally devised force-field analysis as a model for managing change. He argues that change is brought about when the driving force for change exerts greater pressure than the restraining forces that resist it. The change that results is caused by this interaction. The tendency for those who want change is to push for it, but this is likely to invite resistance. Lewin developed force-field analysis to help find other ways to bring about change. He suggests that a better way to bring about change might be to lower the resistance rather than to increase the pressure. Force-field analysis helps identify ways to do this.

Force-field analysis can, in fact, be used to resolve a far wider range of problems. It is a useful technique to use if you are faced with a challenge that you are not certain you can meet fully. Perhaps you want to increase your market share, or persuade senior management to expand your department. Maybe you want to put together a

---

Individual technique: problem solving

Developed by Kurt Lewin, this is a kind of variation on the traditional "listing the pros and cons" approach to problem solving. It helps you to define the challenge, identify your strengths and weaknesses, and then do something about it.

presentation that will help win you a new contract, or perhaps you want to sell off part of the business for the best possible price. Force-field analysis can help you to assess whether a plan is worth pursuing or, if you have already decided to pursue it, force-field analysis can help you improve it.

Force-field analysis forces you to identify the plus and minus factors in the challenge – all the forces acting on it, both positive and negative. Then you can examine how you can swing the balance further in your favor by:

- maximizing your strengths; and/or
- minimizing your weaknesses; and/or
- adding more positive factors.

The steps

1. The first thing to do is to draw up two lists: all the positive forces in one and all the negative forces in the other.
2. Now draw a diagram showing these two lists in columns either side of a central divide, and show the tug-of-war between them.
3. Use this diagram to look for ways to reduce the divide.

Imagine that you plan to launch a big Web site that will give information and invite customers to order from you on the Net. Your force-field analysis might look like Table 1.

The next step is to look for ways to reduce the resistance to change, increase the pressure, or add more positive factors, since any of these will swing the balance in favor of change. This is shown in Table 2.

A popular adaptation involves allocating a score, from 1 (weak) to 5 (strong), to each force. This way you can establish a numerical assessment of the balance of forces on either side. You could do this as in the third table. Initially the forces for change come to 10 points, and the forces against total 11 points.

Table 1

Forces for change	Forces against change
Customers want to make contact via the Net	Cost
It will improve the speed of processing orders	Disruption
Once established it will be very cost effective	Staff frightened of new technology
Competitors are increasing business on the Net	Staff fear of losing jobs

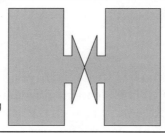

Table 2

Forces for change	Forces against change
Customers want to make contact via the Net	Cost
It will improve the speed of processing orders	Phase in changeover slowly to reduce disruption
Once established it will be very cost effective	Train staff to reduce fear of new technology
Competitors are increasing business on the Net	Guarantee staff there will be no job losses
Show staff how new skills will benefit them	

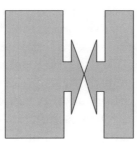

Table 3

	Forces for change		Forces against change	
4	Customers want to make contact via the Net		Cost	3
3	It will improve the speed of processing orders		Disruption	2
1	Once established it will be very cost effective		Staff frightened of new technology	3
2	Competitors are increasing business on the Net		Staff fear of losing jobs	3

Once the forces against change have been reduced, however, the equation swings much more strongly in favor of change (12:7), even allowing for the additional cost of staff training, as in the fourth table.

Example

Force-field analysis can be broadened to analyze challenges and plans other than those which involve managing change. In this case, rather than putting forces for and against change at the top of the columns, simply put positive and negative forces.

Let's suppose you want to put together a big presentation, and you're concerned you won't pull it off successfully. By using force-field analysis, you can identify your chances of success, and then take action to improve them, listing the positive and negative forces, as in Table 4.

Now have a look and see whether any of the positive forces can be enhanced further, new positive forces added, or negative forces reduced. How about bringing in a professional coach to train the presenters to improve their skills and stop them being so nervous? And if your own managers are uninspiring as presenters, perhaps you could ask a charismatic manager from another part of the company to take a lead role in presenting. As for the script, you could go on a course in presentation skills and learn how to improve it yourself. Now your force-field analysis should look more like the Table 5.

Table 4

	Forces for change		Forces against change	
4	Customers want to make contact via the Net		Cost	4
3	It will improve the speed of processing orders		Phase in changeover slowly to reduce disruption	1
1	Once established it will be very cost effective		Train staff to reduce fear of new technology	1
2	Competitors are increasing business on the Net		Guarantee staff there will be no job losses	1
2	Show staff how new skills will benefit them			

Table 5

Positive forces	Negative forces
Strong and convincing case to put across	Limited time to prepare
Well structured format	Inexperienced and nervous presenters
Comfortable budget	Section managers uninspiring as presenters
Good venue with all necessary facilities	Poorly written script
Good design team for visual aids	

Your big presentation now looks more likely to succeed. You have reduced the negative forces, and added to the positive ones, to create a far more promising scenario (see Table 6).

Table 6

Positive forces	Negative forces
Strong and convincing case to put across	Limited time to prepare
Well structured format	Use professional coach to improve presenters' skills
Comfortable budget	Import charismatic manager to take part
Good venue with all necessary facilities	Train to improve own script writing skills
Good design team for visual aids	
Professional trainer on board to train presenters	

Gordon/Little Technique

One of the biggest blocks to creativity is being too close to the problem you're trying to solve. This can make it impossible to see the wood for the trees, and tends to generate only trite and obvious ideas. Back in 1961, William Gordon, of the Arthur D Little consulting firm, came up with this technique to get around this common problem.

The broad idea is to pull back as far from the problem as possible by looking at the most abstract expression of it you can find. So, for example, instead of asking the question "how can we cut our delivery times from two weeks to 48 hours?" you simply ask:

- "How can we make our customers happy?"
- After exploring the answers to this question, you make it a little more specific: "How can we give good customer service?"
- Generate answers to this and then become more specific still: "What do customers want from a delivery service?"

Group technique: problem solving

When you can't see the woods for the trees, this technique uses an abstract approach to help find creative solutions.

- Finally, state the real question: "How can we cut our delivery times from two weeks to 48 hours?" and generate ideas in the light of the answers to the previous questions.

Three levels of decreasing abstraction before you restate the original question is generally about right, but of course you can vary this if you wish.

The role of the leader in this technique is important, since it is their job to encourage the group to think in big, broad terms, and to pose questions that help towards this. As the questions become more concrete, it is increasingly important to keep this creative mood going, and to arrive at the final problem with a more open mind than usual.

It often works well to keep the group in the dark about the real problem at issue until the last part of the session. However this is often not possible, and often group members will guess by the second or third level of abstraction what they are there to resolve.

Example

Here's an example to illustrate how the answers to abstract questions can help to illuminate a more concrete question. Say your problem is that you have a very high level of absenteeism and you need to find ways to reduce it. Begin by asking the group a very abstract question: "How do you get people to do what you want them to?" The answers might include:

- pay them;
- bribe them;
- make it fun for them;
- threaten them;
- trick them; and
- persuade them.

For your next question, moving slightly closer to the real problem, you could ask: "What makes people want to do something?" Ideas might include:

- they enjoy it;
- it makes them feel important;
- it brings a financial reward;
- it makes them feel physically good;
- it makes them feel part of a social group; and
- it earns them praise.

The final level of abstraction might be: "Why do people come to work?" The list of ideas might look something like this:

- they need the money;
- they enjoy it;
- they like to see their friends at work; and
- they want an excuse to get out of the house.

Having been through all these stages, you can now tell the group the real question – "How can we reduce absenteeism?" – and ask them to generate ideas in the light of their answers to the previous questions. Here are a few possibilities, and the earlier ideas that sparked them:

- Rearrange workstations so that people are better able to talk to their colleagues (help them to feel part of a social group).
- Reward the people with the best attendance records by upgrading job titles (make them feel important).
- Pay people an attendance bonus for very low absenteeism (bribe them).
- Organize some kind of lottery or bingo style continuous competition. If you don't turn up, you can't collect that day's lucky number (make it fun for them).
- Introduce flexitime so that people can work when it suits them best (give them an excuse to get out of the house).

- Improve break time facilities: add a gym (make them feel physically good) and a comfortable rest room (they like to see their friends).
- Post a list each month of those people who have made a hundred percent attendance (give them praise).
- Paint the place in bright colors, have fun motivational meetings at the start of the day, play games at work (make it fun for them).

Involving An Outsider

H ave you ever noticed that when someone calls you up and says "I'm after ideas for something, could you think about it and call me back?", somehow the ideas never flow well. However, if the same person calls you and says "Have you got five minutes? I'm after some ideas," between the two of you, you often find that ideas come tumbling out.

Some people resist asking for input from others as though it is an admission of their inability to solve the problem on their own. In fact, however, it produces results you couldn't generate on your own, because the other person provides a creative stimulus. The combination of two minds is greater than the sum of its parts.

Individual technique: problem solving/idea generation

The time-honored practice of asking for advice or input from someone else might seem incongruous at first in this book, but it can be one of the most creative – and simplest – ways to solve problems or generate ideas.

Who to ask

One of the most important aspects of this creative technique is knowing who to ask. Of course, you can consult as many people as you like, but the most efficient approach is to ask the most potentially productive. And who you ask depends on what you want from them.

Expert advice

The most common, but arguably least creative, application of this technique is to go to an expert. Find someone who is a professional or who has encountered your problem before. In this case you are not really asking for new ideas; merely for existing ideas which you are unaware of but the expert will know. In fact, experts can sometimes be less creative than others because they are too closely involved in the problem.

Experience in one part of the problem

Perhaps you have a sticky problem to resolve with your staff, which involves great diplomacy. You could try asking someone who knows little about dealing with staff but a great deal about diplomacy. How about asking a nurse? Or a police officer? Their different perspective still incorporates the core skills you need to draw on, and can stimulate a creative new approach.

Diplomacy is not the only skill you might want to call on. Perhaps you know someone with no technical understanding of your problem but a very methodical, logical mind which might help you to find the solution you want. Some people are notable for their empathetic understanding of human emotions, or their natural grasp of physics, or their intuitive ability to solve problems. When you feel you need outside input, think about what it is you want, and then consult someone with the skills you've identified.

Neutrality

There are times when the problem in question is very controversial, and arouses strong feelings. Should you merge two departments into one? How can you extend the premises into the car park without removing most employees' parking spaces? Which staff are going to have to be laid off? In these circumstances, the important thing is to find someone neutral, who will be more open to finding creative solutions than those who have their own agenda. Being relaxed about the subject will open them up to ideas that someone tense and hung up on the issue is unlikely to come up with.

Distance from the problem

Sometimes you are wrestling with a problem and you're quite sure the answer is staring you in the face, but you just can't see it. In this sort of situation, it helps to find someone who is not involved in the problem at all and who may be able to see what you simply can't. A friend, partner or even a child will often help you to solve this sort of problem creatively.

High level creativity

Some people have naturally quirky, creative minds. Cultivate these people, and consult them when you encounter the kind of problem which you feel needs a really radical or off-the-wall solution.

Getting the best from other people

There is an art to getting the best input from outsiders. As well as cultivating a list of friends, colleagues, ex-colleagues, family and so on to consult when you need outside help, you also need to ask in the right way to get the best response.

Take their time

As a creative technique, asking an outsider doesn't simply mean getting someone else's ideas. It means combining someone else's ideas with your own to produce a creative merger of ideas. To do this, you need to interact. So it's no good stating your problem and asking someone to go away, think about it, and then come back with any ideas. You have to talk to them directly. Ask them for a few minutes of their time and, if they are busy, ask for some time later rather than just leaving it with them. By all means tell them what you want to discuss with them, but make sure the end result is an interactive creative session on the phone or face to face.

Don't crowd them with facts

Outsiders are generally useful because they aren't blinded by the problem. You may not be able to see the wood for the trees, but they can. So don't give them unnecessary information. Just give them an outline of the problem. If they ask, or you feel it's needed, you can fill them in with more detail.

There is a great temptation to limit solutions to a problem. It's easy to say "Now so much business is done by phone or on the Net, we need to find a way of streamlining our sales department without redundancies and without moving offices." But perhaps the reason you can't see a workable solution yourself is because you are hung up on avoiding redundancies or an office move. Don't hamstring your outsider in this way, or they will be unable to see anything you can't see yourself. Perhaps the answer lies in voluntary redundancies, or sales staff working from home; ideas which are easier to see if you aren't trying to avoid redundancies or moving offices.

Don't be negative

Bear in mind that an answer that doesn't take account of all the details may be the spark that helps you find a workable solution. So don't be too quick to say "Ah, that couldn't work because ..." Think about how the idea could be adapted to fit the conditions – or how the conditions could be adapted to fit the solution.

Suppose you want to develop a device to help frail or disabled people to pick up your range of heavy saucepans without dropping them. You ask an outsider who suggests a heavy-duty rubber glove with grips on it, which help hold the handle without slipping. Don't rush to say, "That wouldn't work because the handles are hot and they would melt the rubber." How about changing the material from rubber to a heat-resistant fiber? Or redesigning the saucepans to incorporate handles that don't heat up? The reason you're asking someone else is in order to find a new approach to a solution, so use it, don't reject it.

Example

Children are a classic source of good ideas when your own dry up. They have a freshness of approach, and are often uncluttered by the knowledge and assumptions which dog the rest of us. Sometimes they can see the obvious when we can't.

A salesman for Panasonic provided some sample camcorders for the kids to play with at his son's birthday party. While they were using them, he asked some of the kids for ideas for improving them. One of the kids said they were great, but wanted one for left handers. Until then, no one had marketed a camcorder that was suitable for left handers but, as a result of this suggestion, Panasonic developed a camcorder with a viewfinder that swiveled to accommodate both right and left handers.

Left-brain/Right-brain Thinking

T he brain is divided into two hemispheres, right and left, which meet in a central band of fibers that transfers information between them, known as the *corpus callosum*. The right and left hemispheres each have their own mode of thinking and, although we all use both sides of the brain, most of us favor one more than the other. The right brain is essentially creative and the left brain analytical.

What is more, if you use both sides of the brain at once the two modes of processing interfere with each other, reducing their potential performance. So the most productive way of thinking is to use your own favored side of the brain, and think in a way which doesn't attempt to use the other side. In other words, think purely creatively with no thought for logic or practicality, or be analytical and objective and forget about coming up with original ideas altogether. This technique does just that.

Group technique: idea generation

The two hemispheres of the brain utilize different styles of thinking – one creative and non-verbal, the other logical and analytical. This technique maximizes each and then brings the two together to generate creative yet workable ideas.

Of course, there is a sense in which this is cringingly oversimplified, but it is clear and helpful for the purpose of generating ideas; if you want to train your staff up to take degrees in neurology, you'll need to go into more detail. Obviously you can't shut down either side of the brain completely; you will still need to speak and write for example, and to use your brain for all sorts of unconscious functions. But you can maximize your use of one side of the brain, and minimize your use of the other.

The stages

Step 1

The first stage of this technique is for everybody taking part to identify whether they are predominantly a left-brain or a right-brain thinker. There are questionnaires and tests to establish this, but for the purpose of this technique they are unnecessary. Most people know perfectly well which side of the brain they favor (and so do their colleagues), once they understand the difference, and that's good enough for this exercise.

So what's the difference? Well, left-brain thinking is logical, analytical, verbal, linear, non-artistic. Right-brain thinking, by contrast, is creative, artistic, emotional, non-linear. The table below gives a clear picture of the difference: if you show it to a group, almost everybody will identify more with one than the other.

Step 2

Once everybody has decided which side of the brain they favor, divide them into two groups. Put all the left-brain dominant people in one group, and all the right-brain dominant people in the other group. This works best with a good half dozen or so people in each group.

Left-brain	Right-brain
Verbal	Non-verbal
Analytical	Holistic
Intellectual	Intuitive
Linear	Non-linear
Objective	Subjective
Sequential	Multiple
Rational	Emotional
Directed	Free
Concrete	Abstract
Convergent	Divergent
Structured	Flexible
Logical	Musical
Mathematical	Creative
Speaking	Visual-pictorial
Pattern user	Pattern seeker
Judgemental	Non-judgemental
Orderly	Disorderly
Literal	Metaphorical

Step 3

Now instruct the groups to come up with ideas that address the focal question. Ask the left-brain group to generate as many practical, rational, conventional ideas as they can. Ask the right-brain group to come up with bizarre, wacky and non-rational ideas. Give the groups about 15 to 20 minutes for this part of the exercise, and have at least two people in each group record the ideas.

Step 4

Once the two groups have come up with as many ideas as they can, swap half the people in each group over, so that each group now contains half left-brain and half right-brain thinkers. Each group should have a copy of each of the two lists – left-brain ideas and right-brain ideas.

Step 5

The groups should now combine ideas from the two lists and use these combinations to generate new ideas. One of the most productive ways to combine ideas is to take one idea at random from each list and find ways to combine the two you've selected (but the left-brain thinkers will probably want to find a more methodical method).

Example

Let's imagine you want to come up with new designs and features for your range of lawnmowers. Your left-brain group might suggest ideas such as:

A   make the handle a more comfortable shape;
B   develop a more reliable engine;
C   use a blade which cuts even lower;
D   give the lawnmower a tighter turning circle; and
E   create a more durable outer casing.

Meanwhile, your right-brain thinkers might come up with:

F   design a lawnmower which cuts grass clippings so finely they can be spread on the lawn without being visible;
G   have a detachable strimmer on the side of the mower to strim banks and edges as you mow;
H   develop a lawnmower that can tell when you run it across the grass whether it needs mowing; and
I   design a mower that is powered by rotted compost.

Combining one idea from each group at random, let's look at some possible combination ideas:

B/F   make a lawnmower that shaves the grass rather than rotating a blade;

C/H   put a sensor on the blade so that it stops if it doesn't sense grass at the height it is set at;

A/G   Design a mower with a matching strimmer that clips securely on to the handle so you can carry it around with you;

D/F   collect the clippings in a cylinder which sprays them out in a wide arc instead of depositing them in lumps; and

E/I   compress and collect the grass clippings in a cylinder mounted on the casing, which adds composting fluid from a refillable reservoir. When the clippings are emptied they will be ready to compost down faster.

Lotus Blossom Technique

T his is a popular method of generating ideas in a group, since it flows fast from one theme to another. However, it is also a useful technique to use on your own. The lotus blossom technique is helpful at the beginning of a process to generate lots of ideas to work on, and it is also valuable in finding new applications for existing products or technologies – this is something the Japanese are very good at, and the technique was developed in Japan.

It was developed by Yasuo Matsumura, president of Clover Management Research, and is sometimes known as the MY method after his Japanese initials. Lotus blossom petals – like many other flowers – radiate out from the center. In this technique, ideas radiate out from the center following the same pattern. These ideas, in turn, become the center of a new lotus blossom.

Individual or group technique: idea generation

This technique replicates the structure of the lotus flower. It takes a central theme and finds ideas for it. Each of these ideas then becomes a central theme with more ideas radiating out from it, and so on.

See also: Attribute listing, Mind mapping.

The steps

6	3	7	6	3	7	6	3	7
2	F	4	2	C	4	2	G	4
5	1	8	5	1	8	5	1	8
6	3	7	F	C	G	6	3	7
2	B	4	B		D	2	D	4
5	1	8	E	A	H	5	1	8
6	3	7	6	3	7	6	3	7
2	E	4	2	A	4	2	H	4
5	1	8	5	1	8	5	1	8

1. Start by writing your central theme or issue in the center of the MY lotus blossom diagram shown here.
2. In each of the eight squares around the central square, write a related idea. If you are working in a group, you can brainstorm these eight ideas.
3. Now transfer these eight ideas to the central squares of the outer ring of boxes, and surround each one with another eight ideas.
4. If you wish, you can repeat the process, with any of these ideas at the center of a lotus flower.

5. You will inevitably find, especially if you radiate out more than twice, that your ideas begin to dry up. Even two iterations, as you can see, will generate 64 ideas. If you used every one of these as the center of a new lotus flower you would give yourself scope for a further 512 ideas. So be realistic. After the basic two iterations, create new boxes for only the most promising ideas, and aim simply to fill in as many squares as you can.

Instead of writing eight ideas around the central box, you might prefer to list eight attributes of a product or problem. So if you are looking for new ideas for designing telephones, you might list: receiver, handset, buttons, ringer, memory, special features, casing, sound quality. You can then brainstorm ideas around each of these.

Example

Imagine your central theme is washing machine. You manufacture them and you are looking for new ideas to develop. The items surrounding washing machine might well be those shown here.

F Plumbing	C Detergent	G Program selector
B Loading door	WASHING MACHINE	D Special washes
E Temperature	A Spin	H Filter

Also shown is a possible outer box generated by detergent.

6 Impregnated sheets of detergent	3 Put detergent straight in the drum	7 Filter out chemicals before draining
2 Fill up reservoir and it lasts for 20 washes	DETERGENT	4 No-detergent wash for freshen-up
5 Load dispenser and put into the drum	1 Tablets	8 Attach bottle straight on to machine

Each of the other seven outer boxes would have eight ideas around them. You could take any of the most promising ideas, such as number 8: attach bottle straight on to machine, and generate a further eight ideas radiating out from this.

Mind Mapping

I f you are using the creative right side of your brain, you inhibit its potential by using the logical left side strongly at the same time; the more you focus your thinking in one hemisphere, the more productively it works. So it stands to reason that if you are trying to think creatively you don't want to focus your left brain on recording your ideas in a structured, logical manner.

Mind mapping is a right-brain approach to recording ideas. But it is more than that: it also helps you to generate ideas because it gives your creative mind free rein. It encourages you to let go of boundaries and structures and to think expansively.

Individual technique: idea generation

Developed in the mid-70s by Tony Buzan, mind maps are a visual and free-form method of developing ideas using right-brain thinking. They use association literally to draw connections between ideas and create a map of a subject.

See also: Attribute listing, Brainstorming, Left-brain/right-brain thinking, Lotus blossom technique.

Tony Buzan originally developed this technique for note taking, but it soon became apparent that it works extremely well for generating new ideas. What is more, although it records ideas – and is useful for this in brainstorming, for example – you rarely need to refer to it again because you will find that you remember it so clearly.

The steps

If you haven't encountered mind mapping before, you'll have to read this description in tandem with the following diagram or it will make no sense. The basic gist of mind mapping is to begin with a central theme, encapsulated as a key word, which you write in the center of your page. (Most people prefer to turn an A4 sheet round so it is in landscape format.) You can draw a circle or box around this key word, or any shape you like. If the key word is packaging, you might want to draw a 3-D cube around it. If it is accommodation, you might draw a house, and so on.

Now draw lines leading from this central theme as you generate ideas, and along each one write any other key words relating to the theme which spring to mind. Or you might prefer to write the keyword with a box or circle round it, and link this to the central key word with a line.

You can write other words and ideas related to these key words beside them, or in lines leading off them, or whatever works for you. Just keep going, linking and relating ideas until you have run out.

The rules

There aren't any rules. Your right brain does its own thing, and the aim is to give it as much freedom as possible. As with brainstorming, anything goes. Get the ideas down first, and worry later about how useful each one is. You can write the satellite key words first, and then work on the ideas leading off from them. Or just write one of them down and explore that before you move on to the next. You can jump around the page, jotting ideas down as you think of them. You can create subsidiary groups of words leading from other groups, which lead in turn from other groups. You can write ideas down anywhere on the page you like; don't worry about putting them in the 'right' place. Just make sure you get your ideas down and explore them.

Use as many techniques as you can to get the information down in a way that suits you. You might:

- use drawings and symbols;
- color code ideas;
- use a highlighter pen to indicate e.g. take action on this now or get more info;
- use capital letters for some ideas;
- use larger or smaller writing for different ideas; and
- use arrows to connect ideas.

Some people never get to grips with mind mapping – the lack of logical structure just doesn't suit them. But huge numbers of people who learn the technique continue to use it. And everyone has their own style. Some people produce very colorful mind maps, others don't color code but have pictures everywhere, some mind maps are neat and use only words, some are a mess with icons and personal symbols everywhere.

Example

Here is an example of a mind map, which explores the idea of mind mapping. A mind map is very subjective, and the process of creating it is often more important than the map itself. Using someone else's mind map just doesn't work. So the example shown here will illustrate what a mind map is, but you will find it easier to follow this text than to learn about mind mapping from the map itself.

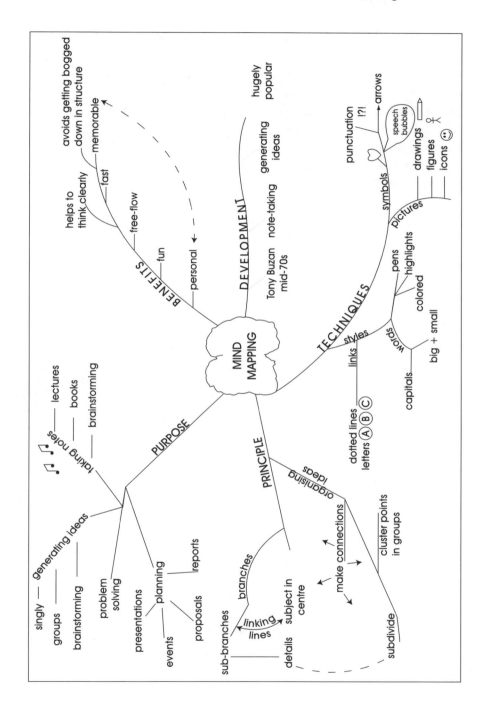

All sorts of successful business people swear by mind mapping. Among many others the engineer responsible for Boeing's technical publications unit keeps notes on everything he needs to know as a series of mind maps in a spiral bound notebook. He also has a 40 × 4 foot mind map he once produced, displayed on his wall.

Others use mind maps to help them decide how and when to sack employees, to develop presentations or proposals, to predict future trends, to explore new markets and to develop new products and services. Try it.

Morphological Analysis

T his technique is credited to Fritz Zwicky who devised it in the mid-60s, although many minor variations on it have been developed since. It is particularly useful for modifying products or services, or developing new ones.

The basic idea, and the simplest version, is to list attributes of a product or service across the top of a grid. Below each, list all the variations you can think of for that attribute. So if you run a picture framing business and want to develop new product and service variations, you might list: frame, glass, picture, delivery. Under each, allow yourself as many boxes as you like; five is about right for a simple analysis. In each, list all the variations of the attribute above that you can think of (see table).

Individual/group technique: idea generation

Morphology is the study of structure and form, and this technique helps you to generate ideas by creating new combinations of attributes.

See also: Attribute listing, Forced relationship, Verbal checklist.

Frame	Glass	Picture	Delivery
Plastic	Clear	Customer's own	Customer collect
Wood	Perspex	Chosen from range	Deliver to customer
Metal	Non-reflective	Own photograph	Post/courier
Board	"Soft-focus" finish	Photo-montage	Gift delivery
Glass	No glass	Commission	Self-assembly

Now all you have to do is take one idea from each column – chosen at random – and use the combination to spark off new ideas. Go through this process several times and see how many good ideas you come up with.

For example, you might select: board, perspex, customer's own picture, self-assembly. You could sell DIY picture framing kits in materials people can easily cut to size themselves.

Or you might select: glass, non-reflective, photo-montage, gift delivery. You could sell classy, glass-framed montages of customers' own photos and then gift package them and deliver them to an address of the customer's choice. So people could send their parents a collection of photos of the grandchildren, or send someone a montage of photos of their favorite pets or cars or gardens.

Variations

You don't have to stick to listing variations of the attributes you use. You can create a grid, which lists attributes along one axis and change words along the other. Change words might be verbs, adverbs or adjectives, such as multiply, enlarge, shrink, combine, modify and so on. In this case, you would pick a square on the grid at random, and read off the entries on the two axes to generate an idea.

If you use ten attributes and ten change words, you should be able to generate a hundred ideas. As with many creative techniques, quantity is the important thing to begin with; the more ideas you generate, the more high quality ideas you'll end up with. In the example shown, the product being considered is a food processor.

Attributes										
Base unit										
Lead										
Switch										
Bowl									z	
Lid				y						
Locking device										
Motor										
Blade							x			
Beater										
Whisk										
Change words	Enlarge	Modify	Shrink	Omit	Switch round	Merge	Add to	Detach	Inside out	Break up

- You might pick box x and combine *blade* and *add to*. Perhaps a rotating unit with four rather than two blades would be more efficient?
- If you select box y you combine *lid* and *omit*. How about a sliding top on the bowl rather than a separate lid?
- Box z gives you *bowl* and *inside out*. Maybe you could design a flexible bowl that you can turn inside out in order to remove the food more completely after processing.

3-D morphology

This variation entails using a matrix with three axes, which gives you a huge range of possible ideas – a ten by ten by ten matrix would produce 1000 ideas. You can list attributes on all three axes so you combine three attributes rather than two. This is similar to the forced relationship technique where, for example, you would generate an idea from the attributes whisk, lid and base unit. (Maybe you could have a whisk spinning on a vertical rod that is attached to the lid at the top and the base unit at the bottom.)

You don't have to list attributes on all three axes. You might list attributes on one, change words on another and questions on a third: for example, you might use the matrix above but add a third axis listing: who, where, what, when, why, how.

The third axis might list, according to your product or service, colors, materials, company departments or anything else you think is a relevant variable to generate ideas with. If this sounds rather complicated to put down on paper, there are software programs that help you to enumerate the combinations, and will give you random combinations to use (see p. 190).

Nominal Group Technique

T he nominal group technique (NGT) is intended for small groups. It differs from most other group techniques in that there is very little interaction between group members. What's the point of that, you might ask. Well, there are times when you want to minimize interaction because it may lead to conflict, or particularly when one person is likely to dominate the group and thereby the outcome of the session. Some people dominate through force of personality, but sometimes it is the presence of someone of authority that dominates the rest of the group. Whatever the reason, NGT circumvents the problem.

It should be said, on the minus side, that the lack of interaction of course removes some of the creative spark. Group interaction makes creative sessions more fun and allows people to piggy-back on the ideas of their colleagues. But NGT certainly has a place when

---

Group technique: problem solving

This technique derives its name from the fact that the group is a group in name only. This is a non-interactive approach to solving problems in small groups.

See also: Delphi technique.

you reckon that the group is unlikely to interact in a positive way for some reason.

The technique restricts discussion of ideas to a simple explanation where necessary, and group members then vote for ideas by secret ballot. It works well with fairly narrowly defined problems such as developing strategy. At the end of the NGT session you will have chosen a solution, and it is important that all group members accept the decision of the group as final.

The stages

There are four key stages in NGT: generating written ideas, recording ideas, clarifying ideas and voting on ideas.

Stage 1 – Generating written ideas

The group leader defines the problem being addressed, and writes it on a flipchart or board for everyone to view. Each group member, without discussion, writes down all their ideas in a five or ten minute period.

Stage 2 – Recording ideas

The ideas are recorded, round-robin fashion, on the flipchart or board, without discussion. The leader asks each person in turn to give one idea from their list that has not already been given by someone else. This continues around the group until everyone has exhausted their list and all the ideas are recorded in view of the group.

Stage 3 – Clarifying ideas

Before the group can vote on the ideas, it is important to make sure that everyone understands them all. So this stage consists of working through every item on the list, in the order they were recorded, and asking the group if they have any questions. If anyone is unclear about what any of the ideas mean, the person who put forward the idea explains it. They should take a maximum of one minute to clarify the meaning of the idea. However, the object is not to sell the idea – simply to explain it. The merits of the idea should not be discussed, but group members can ask questions to help them understand.

Stage 4 – Voting on ideas

It is not uncommon to come up with 50 or even 100 ideas in a nominal group session. So the next stage is to vote for the group's best choice. You can choose your own voting system, but here is the most popular. Each participant writes down what they consider to be the top five ideas on an index card. They rank these from one to five, allocating five points to their favorite idea through to one point for the least favorite of the five. These cards are all handed to the leader, who adds up the points for each idea and announces the top ideas. Occasionally one clear favorite emerges, but generally it is necessary to hold a second round of voting.

In the second round, the leader announces the top five to ten ideas (it is often clear which are the front runners). The voting process is repeated, but this time participants vote for their top two or three choices only. Again, their favorite idea should be allocated two or three points, and their least favorite selection only one.

Variation

The Improved Nominal Group Technique combines NGT with the Delphi technique (see p. 65). Its aim is to preserve the anonymity of the person submitting each idea, so there is no scope for personal loyalties or animosity to interfere in the process. To achieve this, everyone submits their ideas in advance of the meeting, with any necessary explanation, so that the session can pick up at stage three with the leader reading out any explanations needed to clarify the ideas. The group then goes straight into the first round of voting.

NGT in action

Suppose a strong new competitor has emerged on the market. You need to decide on a strategy for dealing with this threat. However, you know from informal discussion that factions are emerging among your managers. Some feel strongly that resources should go into strengthening your market position, while others are insistent that you must diversify into other markets in order to survive.

An open meeting is likely to prove unpleasant and divisive. It will probably achieve little, and may well create all sorts of people problems you could well do without. What is more, the more junior managers will worry about who they are seen to support, and this may influence the position they adopt.

This situation is ideal for NGT. You may even wish to use the improved version so that the ideas submitted are anonymous. All the issues are likely to be debated and argued informally before the meeting, so the arguments won't need reiterating.

Of course, this kind of new strategy will need open debate and decision making at some stage, but not necessarily now. You can take as the theme of the session: where should we invest our resources to counter the threat of new competition? This, after all, is the area of intense disagreement. Once this question is resolved, you can discuss the next stage – the detail – more amicably.

Your managers may have a number of ideas. Those who support diversification will presumably have some basic idea of how to diversify. Those who favor strengthening your market position will doubtless have broad ideas as to how this could be achieved. Some managers may have new ideas they have not felt able to voice before. All these ideas should be listed and recorded. The subsequent vote should make it possible for people to register their views honestly and for a majority view to come through clearly.

For a key strategic decision such as this, you may feel that more formal debate is needed if opposing views emerge in close competition. But more often you will find that there is a clear majority, and this is an effective and fair way to identify it. For issues which are less critical, if equally emotive, NGT can be used even where the opposing factions are more evenly matched.

Pattern Language

S ome of us find it easier to be creative if we are free from the constraints of verbal language. Even those of us who are very verbal thinkers can find that our creative mind is opened up if we look at ideas visually for a change. The right side of the brain is the creative side, and also the side where visual skills are located, so it is often effective to use pictures rather than words when trying to think creatively.

Pattern language was originally developed by architects Alexander, Ishikawa and Silverstein to help create new building designs. It is a useful technique for finding creative solutions to sticky problems, or for finding new products or new applications for products. If you get on well with it, it can become a regular technique; if you are more of a verbal thinker by preference, try pattern language when verbal thinking doesn't seem to be getting you anywhere.

Individual technique: problem solving/idea generation

Sometimes your brain responds better to visual than to verbal stimulation. Pattern language takes the attributes of a problem and translates them into abstract symbols.

See also: Attribute listing, Drawing techniques.

The principle behind pattern language is simple. Instead of trying to express the elements of a problem or challenge verbally, and then looking for connections between the words, which will spark ideas, you do the same thing using patterns and symbols.

The stages

Start by listing the attributes of your problem or subject. For example, suppose you are trying to find a way of speeding up the progress of queues through checkouts in your stores. You might list the attributes of the process as:

* checkout assistant;
* customers;
* speed;
* trolleys;
* conveyor belt;
* movement;
* barcode reader;
* till;
* bags;
* money;
* purse; and
* receipt.

Now draw a graphic symbol of each attribute on an index card. Write the attribute on the back of the card. It doesn't matter whether you can draw or not, and it doesn't matter if the symbol you draw would make no sense to anyone else – it has nothing to do with them. The technique is for your benefit alone. Don't spend too long thinking about the symbol, just allow it to evolve naturally. The act of drawing the symbols is the first stage of letting go and opening up your intuitive, creative responses. The diagram overleaf shows some examples of symbols to illustrate the attributes of the checkout process.

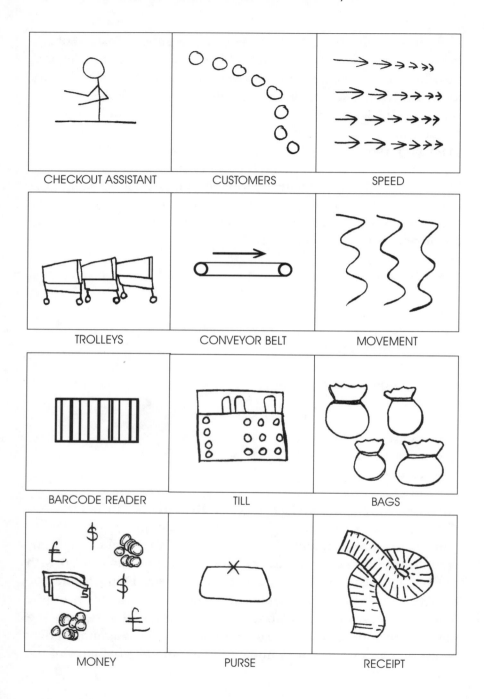

CHECKOUT ASSISTANT CUSTOMERS SPEED

TROLLEYS CONVEYOR BELT MOVEMENT

BARCODE READER TILL BAGS

MONEY PURSE RECEIPT

If the attributes of your particular problem are more abstract, the symbols will be more symbolic, of course, like the ones illustrated here for speed and movement. For example, you might want to create symbols for different departments on your organization, such as distribution, marketing, accounts or production. What do they mean to you? Distribution might be an envelope, or a map of the region with arrows on it, or a lorry. Marketing might be a simple representation of a street market, or a newspaper, or someone on a platform talking to lots of other people. Just draw whatever comes to mind and feels appropriate to you.

Now spread out all the cards on the desk with the symbols facing up. Move them around. Mix and match symbols randomly. Just take two or three cards and focus on them, and perhaps add others in turn. Don't try to force anything; just move the cards around intuitively.

You might find that you come up with ideas or quickly, or you might want to use other techniques such as free association (see p. 21) or forced relationship (see p. 86) to stimulate ideas. If your ideas start to dry up, try adding more symbols – for the example above you could add anything you personally associate with checkout queues, for example:

- car keys;
- small children;
- chatter;
- food;
- groceries;
- pen;
- chequebook;

... and so on. Your ideas may well come from seeing something completely different in a symbol from what you originally meant by it. For example, you might use an asterisk to symbolize a taboo subject, and then see it as a star and use that idea to spark off ideas. So be as open to inspiration as possible; it doesn't matter where good ideas come from, just so long as they come.

The checkout symbols could stimulate all sorts of ideas. For example:

- The symbols for customers, barcode reader and receipt all suggest a long line or strip divided into separate units. Maybe you need more types of checkout. Not just 5 items or less and cash only, but also checkouts for no items to be weighed and customers with children (with toys or video screens to entertain the kids in the queues) and 20 items or less.
- The checkout assistant symbol calls to mind someone singing or dancing. How about making queueing more entertaining so customers don't mind the time it takes? Employ a stand-up comic to amuse customers, or hold a sing-song (you could combine this with the last idea and have, say, half a dozen checkouts at one end of the store for entertainments). Or just have posters with quiz questions or mind puzzles on them, which are changed every week.
- The customers symbol together with the symbol for speed suggests two different modes of queueing: one queue per checkout, or a single queue as you might get in a bank or post office. How about all customers joining a single queue and the front person from the queue moving to the next available checkout? Or, if this is impracticable, how about one queue to every half dozen checkouts?
- The conveyor belt symbol looks a bit like a safety-pin. Together with the trolleys symbol this suggests the possibility of having a printed list of purchases pinned to the trolley. The trolley has a lid and the barcode of anything put into the trolley is automatically registered as it goes in. If you change your mind, the barcode registers a subtraction as you take the item out of the trolley. When you arrive at the checkout, the list is simply fed into the till and the total added up. All you have to do is pay; no more conveyor belts.
- The trolleys spark off the idea of railway stations and porters. How about porters who will do all or part of your shopping for you. They wait by the entrance for customers to give them a

shopping list, and shop while the customer sits in the coffee shop, or the customer and the porter do half the shopping each. The queue at the checkout may not be quicker, but the actual shopping process is.

These are just a few ideas to show how stimulating pattern language can be, and what creative ideas it can generate. Forcing your mind to address problems in a whole new way is very liberating and opens up your creative processes.

Example

An excellent example of pattern language at work is the banker who wanted to develop some way of reducing the problem of stolen checks. He decided to use this technique to help him. After drawing a blank several times – with several sets of symbols – he finally saw the solution. It was sparked by the act of using pictures itself. He decided to produce checkbooks with checks that carried a picture of the customer on them.

Problem Reversal

L ike assumption reversal, this is essentially an individual technique, but one that can be adapted very well to group use. Assumption reversal (see p. 26) is an excellent method of generating ideas around a broad question, in which you challenge the assumptions implicit in that question. By contrast, problem reversal focuses on solving a specific problem rather than generating broad ideas, but uses a similar approach to do so.

The stages

The technique is very straightforward, and begins with a clear statement of your problem. For example:

Individual technique: problem solving

This technique turns a problem on its head in order to find a new perspective from which to view it.

See also: Assumption reversal.

---

1. Our supermarket trolleys get stolen too easily.
2. Our accounts department is obstructive towards other departments.
3. Our seasonal ranges of fashion shoes become obsolete too quickly.

Having identified your problem, the next step is to reverse it. You can reverse any part of the problem you like; it doesn't have to be the verb. Now write down your new "problem". It doesn't matter if it makes much sense or not:

1. Our supermarket trolleys get returned too easily.
2. Other departments are obstructive towards our accounts department.
3. Our seasonal ranges of fashion shoes become obsolete too slowly.

Having reversed your problem, simply study the new version and see what ideas it gives you. Work out how you could generate the reversed effect. For example, how would you go about making it "too easy" to return supermarket trolleys? This may lead you to ideas for preventing them being stolen. Another option is to think, "What if …?" What if everyone else was obstructive towards the accounts department? What effect would that have? What would you do about it? Or perhaps you need to consider what everyone else hasn't – this is why the Japanese started making small, fuel-efficient cars, to compete with all the huge gas-guzzlers on the market. Let's have a look at the three examples above and see what solutions the reversal process suggests.

The problems and their solutions

Our supermarket trolleys get returned too easily

How could trolleys be returned so easily? Perhaps there might be a financial reward for returning them, or a refund, or free sweets for the kids. Or they might have some kind of homing device. They could become unusable in some way once they travel beyond 500 yards of the store – perhaps an inbuilt receiver causes the wheels to lock up once it goes out of range of the transmitter at the store. Maybe the trolleys are fixed to a network of tracks on the ground; they can be guided around the store along the tracks, and to any of the car park spaces, but can't go beyond this. All of these ideas could help to reduce theft; instead of trying to punish people who remove trolleys, incentivize people to return them.

Other departments are obstructive towards our accounts department

If this were the case, the accounts department might be given special concessions and help to overcome the problem. Or other departments might be asked to justify their behavior, and to rectify it. This train of thought could lead you to wonder whether the accounts department sees it the same way as everyone else. Perhaps in their eyes it is everyone else who is unhelpful or obstructive, and perhaps you should ask accounts to justify their behavior. Maybe they can, and perhaps they really do need extra support or concessions.

Our seasonal ranges of fashion shoes become obsolete too slowly

What would happen if this were the case? Your R&D department would have to cut back if you didn't bring out new designs so frequently. Production would produce far more units of each design, and this would mean materials could be ordered in greater bulk, and therefore more cheaply. The production schedule would ease off, without the urgency to get the designs in the shops before they became obsolete. Sales staff would have to sell fewer designs, and those they sold would have a much longer shelf life.

Looking at the problem from this perspective, perhaps you should get out of the seasonal fashion shoe market and sell shoes and boots in designs that last longer. After all, the original problem – *our seasonal ranges of fashion shoes become obsolete too quickly* – suggests that you might not be positioned where you are most comfortable in the market. A born fashion shoe producer would probably never consider this a problem in the first place.

Examples

Many companies have done well out of problem reversal. Businesses like Apple Computers have looked at the market and instead of saying "how can we compete with all these big players?" have asked themselves "how can we do what all these other companies aren't doing?"

Alfred Sloan, who took over General Motors in 1946 and turned it around, was a master of problem reversal. One classic example was the problem that people had to buy cars before they could drive them. He pioneered the concept of buying a car in installments, making car ownership accessible to a new market. When he realized that GM had eight models of car which were competing with each other and with everyone else (chiefly Ford), he looked for the opposite approach to resolve the problem. He slimmed down the range to five cars, and targeted each at a different type of consumer. He did this so successfully that you could tell what kind of person someone was by the car they drove.

T here are some creative techniques that involve wacky ideas that shake up your thinking and force you to find links between words like *tapeworm* and *caravan*. These questions aren't like that. They involve straightforward, linear thinking applied directly to your own problem. But the right questions can, nevertheless, lead you to creative solutions.

There are two standard questioning techniques that are widely used in creative thinking: asking why, and the six basic questions.

Asking why

This is a quick and simple approach, which anyone who has ever had

---

Individual technique: problem solving

The key to finding the right answer to your problem is finding the right question. Often you find that asking comparatively simple questions leads you to answers you might not otherwise have found.

See also: Verbal checklist.

small children will already know intimately. It entails asking the question "why?" until you get a satisfactory answer. You need to repeat the question five times. The point of this is that it forces you deeper into a problem than you might otherwise go, so the time to use it is when you feel that you haven't really got to the root of the problem.

Suppose the problem is that you have an important report to write and you're so close to the deadline that it's touch and go whether you'll be able to complete it on time. What is the real root of the problem? Start by stating the problem, and then ask "why?" five times. Like this:

I'm not sure I can complete my report on time.

1. Why? – *I've left it almost too late to start.*
2. Why? – *I've been putting it off.*
3. Why? – *I want it to be really impressive, but I don't know what to say.*
4. Why? – *I don't know how to write a report properly.*
5. Why? – *I've never had any training in report writing.*

Aha. So the root of the problem is that you need to enroll on a course, or read a really good book, that will teach you how to write reports professionally. When you see this process written out it seems quite obvious, but it generally isn't so obvious. To take this example, how many people do you know who regularly put off writing reports, and never address the root problem? Maybe the root problem is that they are underconfident about their use of English, or that they dread the response to the report and are in denial about it. It doesn't have to be lack of training. But asking why five times would uncover the root cause so that they could address it.

The six basic questions

When you're developing a new product, service or process, some of the most obvious questions sometimes get missed. This can lead to problems later on. To use a genuine example, suppose you are constructing the world's biggest Ferris wheel on the bank of the River Thames to celebrate the new millennium. In amongst everything else, you forget to think through the question: "How will we get the wheel into position?" The result: a fiasco in which the whole country watches in quiet amusement as your Ferris wheel remains suspended, embarrassingly horizontal, across the width of the river.

The good news is that there are only six questions you can ask. Other questions are just variations on these. Rudyard Kipling recorded them in a more memorable form than anyone else:

I keep six honest serving men
(They taught me all I knew);
Their names are What and Why and When
And How and Where and Who.

Simply working through these six questions in relation to your proposed product or process should help you to identify any potential problems or opportunities at an early stage in development. You might simply want to ask the questions in any order, and you can do this in a group session:

- What?
- Where?
- When?
- Who?
- Why?
- How?

Another effective way of going through this process is to write the subject in the middle of the page and then create a mind map around it to build on (see opposite).

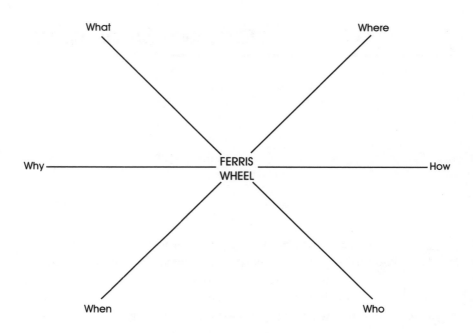

Random Stimulation

T he whole point about creative techniques is that they open your mind up to think in a new way. So if you repeatedly use the same technique, you are defeating the object. That's not to say that it will never work, but it will be less effective because your mind will simply get stuck in a new rut.

Random stimulation is one of the techniques people are most frequently guilty of using too often. But the reason for this is that it's very simple, quick and effective. If you haven't used it before, or haven't used it recently, it is a valuable technique to try. It works well when you feel your thinking about a particular problem or challenge is too rigid, and you want a fresh approach.

Random stimulation is a similar to a less structured form of association (see p. 21) or forced relationship (see p. 86). All you do is

---

Individual technique: problem solving/idea generation

Introducing a completely random element into thinking about a problem or challenge stimulates your mind to find new patterns and connections. This is a very quick, simple and popular technique.

See also: Association, Forced relationship.

take a random word, generally a noun, and think about it. Then relate these thoughts back to your problem, or the product or service you want to develop. It doesn't always work, but then it takes so little time it doesn't matter if it takes a few goes to get a result. It works surprisingly often.

The important thing is to pick a genuinely random word. Don't look for one that you think is going to be productive for the subject in question. Make sure that you arrive at the word by chance. And don't give up on it too quickly. Spend a good five minutes or so thinking about it, and noting down your thoughts, before you decide to try another word or another technique. If you try again with another word, give yourself a break. It can work well to try a fresh word each day until your problem is resolved. If you know that you have to wait a whole day before trying again, it can deter you from giving up too easily on the first word you find.

Choosing a word

The key to random stimulation is choosing a suitable random word. The best words to use are nouns which are simple and which summon up a visual image. You also want words that make you think of lots of other images. For example, the word *water* might make you think of the bath, or washing up, or the sea, or drinks. So if you use one of the techniques for selecting words which involves devising your own list, bear these points in mind – the words should be simple, visual, and stimulate other images.

- You can simply open a dictionary or a newspaper and point with your eyes closed.
- Use a computer program that picks a random word for you (see page 190).
- Write your own list of 60 words. Number these and, when you want to use one, look at the second hand of your watch. Whatever number of seconds it points to is the reference number for the word on your list.

• Keep a bag or box full of random words written on small cards or slips of paper. You can add to these any time you like. When you want a random word, just put your hand in and use the first word you pull out.

In the box is a sample list of 60 words that you might use as the basis of your own list.

---

arm spot roof camera slug lampshade tile fishmonger button zodiac pill screen baby sock biscuit stamp tractor acrobat garage typhoon kiwi engine mountain army flu birthday hockey sweatshirt fridge cat shampoo crowd pudding scanner flour wicket lake café pamphlet toast horseshoe clock magnet eyelashes ink rainforest cream ghost umbrella report wok snakeskin oak armchair wax trolley fire France iceberg timetable

---

Variation

If you prefer, or you want a change, use pictures instead of words. These help stimulate the non-verbal, creative, right-hand side of the brain. Many people find pictures easier to relate to than words.

You can find a random picture by letting a magazine fall open, or an art book, or you could create your own set of picture cards from photographs or postcards, or pictures cut out of magazines. If you create your own set to pick from at random, aim for about sixty images.

You'll find that if you use a picture of a single object, it may not give you much more stimulation than the word for the same object would have done. So try to find pictures with a mood or a story behind them. These can spark off a rich vein of imaginative thought, which can lead to very creative ideas.

Examples

Suppose you are looking for ways to reduce your travelling time between meetings. You select a word at random – let's say it's *octopus*. Think about an octopus for a while:

- it has eight legs;
- it lives in the sea;
- it swims;
- it changes color according to its emotions;
- you can eat it; and
- it has three hearts.

After thinking about the word *octopus* for a while, go back to your original problem with travelling time, and think about the two things together. Can you see any connection? Does the word *octopus* give you any ideas? How about these?

- An octopus has eight legs. If you could be in eight places at once, you would solve a lot of your problems. How about tele-conferencing? Or rescheduling your time so that you arrange appointments and meetings geographically – all your meetings at the office on a Monday, in the city center on a Tuesday, to the north and west of town on a Wednesday and so on.
- What about the fact that an octopus has three hearts? What if you had three locations you worked at, and encouraged as many people as possible to meet you at the one nearest to them. Pick three places that you have to visit from time to time anyway – your office and two other company sites for example.
- Or, thinking about eating octopus, meet people for business lunches. That way you can use the lunchtime you save to travel in, and you still get to eat.

The same word might have given you a completely different set of ideas, but this is an example of how random stimulation can lead you to look at your problem or challenge in a completely new way.

One excellent, real life example of random stimulation is the development of distortion-free glass. Alastair Pilkington, of Pilkington Brothers, had spent years trying to find a way of producing glass without distortions. The production method at the time involved passing molten glass through rollers, which created distortions that had to be polished, and the thinking of the time was that the only way to improve the result was to develop better grinding and polishing techniques.

But one evening, Alastair Pilkington was doing the washing up at home. He was daydreaming and watching a bar of Ivory soap floating in the water. He imagined glass floating like the soap, and a sudden realization came to him. He invented a concept called float glass, whereby the glass is made in an oven in which it floats on molten tin. It cools and hardens before the tin, and can then be passed on to the toughening stage of the process without ever going through the rollers which caused the imperfections. The whole grinding and polishing part of the process is redundant, and the glass is distortion-free.

Rice Storm (TKJ method)

A s the name Rice Storm might suggest, this is a Japanese method, also known as the TKJ method. And it is a technique that suits the Japanese approach very well. It focuses on the aims of the group rather than the individuals within it, and preserves the anonymity of the person who has generated each idea. As with most other techniques, this can inhibit creativity because the group members do not spark off each other, but it can be very useful if group commitment and cohesion is needed.

The other great benefit of using the rice storm approach is that it begins with the process of identifying the problem, before going on to look for solutions. Disagreement or misunderstanding about the problem can be one of the causes of failure or friction in a creative

---

Group technique: problem solving/idea generation

This technique is quite complicated, and is divided into two stages: defining the problem and finding a solution. It is an excellent approach for bringing together individual ideas in a way that is acceptable to the whole group.

See also: Storyboarding.

group. Rice storm has two distinct phases: problem definition and problem solution.

Problem definition

1. The group leader gives the group a general theme, which covers the area of the problem. Each person then writes down facts that are pertinent to this on index cards – one fact per card. The facts should be significant, not trivial. Allow about ten minutes for this stage; that should give you up to about twenty facts per person.
2. The leader then collects up all the cards and redistributes them; this ensures anonymity since people aren't working with their own cards.
3. The leader now reads one card aloud, chosen at random.
4. Group members now look through their stack of cards and select any which relate to the card that was read. They read these cards out to the group. All these related cards go into a pile, and the group gives the set a name that encapsulates its essence, and brings together all the cards in the set.
5. This process is repeated until all the cards are grouped into named sets.
6. These sets are then brought together by the same process until a single, all-inclusive set is created and named. This full named set is the group's consensus definition of the problem.

For example, suppose the general problem is that sales are dropping. The facts written on index cards might be such things as:

- The products are less popular than they were.
- Prices have gone up faster than the competition.
- The sales force is demotivated.
- There are lots of competing products on the market.
- Our corporate image is of a company that doesn't care about its customers.
- Advertising is badly targeted.

In a group of, say, ten people, you might end up with about 150 cards. Some of these will be duplications and some closely related. Perhaps the leader starts by reading out a card that says: "Prices have gone up faster than the competition." Group members might now build a set round this card by reading out related facts such as:

- prices are too high;
- our products are no longer competitive;
- the market is very price-sensitive;
- our competitors are keeping prices down;
- our raw materials are too costly;

... and other relevant statements. Once this set is complete, it has to be named. In this case, the name set might be *uncompetitive pricing*. Other name sets might be *poor marketing, demotivated sales force* and so on.

Once all the cards have been grouped into named sets, some of these might be combined again. For example *negative image* and *lack of advertising* might have been combined into *poor marketing*. Eventually, all these named sets have to be brought together into a final group definition of the problem. For example: "The sales force is demotivated by having to sell to customers who see us as uncaring and over-priced."

Problem solution

Having reached consensus about the nature of the problem, the next stage is to find a solution. The process for this is very similar to the process for defining the problem.

1. Group members write down all the solutions they can think of to the problem as defined in about a ten minute period. Again, each idea is written on a fresh index card. The ideas do not have to relate to the previously stated facts, only to the problem definition.

2.   The cards are collected and redistributed.
3.   The leader once again picks a card at random and reads it out.
4.   Group members now read out any related solutions on the cards in front of them and form a set of cards with these related ideas. This set is then given a name.
5.   The process is repeated until all the cards are sorted into sets, each of which has been given a name.
6.   Finally, an all-inclusive solution, which incorporates all the sets, is created and given a name. One way to do this is to ask the group: "What is the essence of these ideas?" and encourage them to come up with suggestions. The leader should then bring these suggestions together into a statement which expresses the solution, and with which everyone is happy.

For example, the initial ideas, which the participants write down, might include:

*   invite customers to a special function;
*   give long-standing customers discounts;
*   send Christmas cards to all customers;
*   set up a customer careline;
*   hold weekly motivational sessions with the sales force;
*   train the sales force to present a caring image; and
*   support key charities and publicize the fact.

Again, you might end up with as many as 15 or 20 ideas per person. These cards would be sorted into groups such as:

*   launch a PR drive;
*   woo customers directly;
*   motivate the sales force; and
*   improve customer communications.

These solution sets can finally brought together by answering the question "What is the essence of these ideas?" The final solution statement might be: "Launch a drive to reinvent our image as a more caring organization."

Variations

You can skip the stage of combining all the problem named sets into a single definition of the problem. You might feel that there is really more than one problem, and to try to combine them would over-simplify. In this case, you could stop the first part of the process with up to half a dozen named problem sets, and then go through the second, solution-finding process for each of them.

Another variation involves drawing. The leader can draw a picture of the problem in front of the group and suggest they use it to help them generate ideas. Or some of the ideas generated could be converted into graphics and the group asked to use these to come up with still more ideas.

Scenarios

I t is essential for all businesses to plan for the future. We all know that. But it isn't always that easy. After all, we have no idea what the future holds. The idea of scenarios is to construct four or five different, plausible models of the future based around key drivers of future development such as changes in competition, new technology, national or international recession and so on.

Scenarios are most commonly used to prepare alternative strategies. This usually involves a SWOT analysis – analyzing the organization's internal and external forces to identify its **S**trengths, **W**eaknesses, **O**pportunities and **T**hreats. The aim is to identify strategies for building strengths and reducing weaknesses, in order to maximize opportunities and minimize threats to the business. Any problem situation that is changing is a candidate for scenarios.

Group technique: idea generation

This technique requires time, and entails thinking about the future of the business. Although the technique involves writing future scenarios, the ideas generated in the process are more important than the scenarios themselves.

By preparing for these future scenarios, you can generate ideas that will give you a competitive edge now, whether or not the future turns out as you anticipated. If you think, for example, that future competition might drive prices down, you are forced to think of ways to pull your own costs down. Even if prices don't go down in the event, you can still reduce your costs.

The stages

1. The first step is to identify your problem. For example: "What impact will developing technology have on the business?" or "How will expanding competition affect pricing policy?" or "What if our core product becomes obsolete?"
2. Next, identify between three and five key drivers which will determine your organization's future, such as the economy, new technology, market structure, cash flow, competition and so on.
3. Now construct a future scenario around each of these key drivers. You need to come up with plausible scenarios such as:

   • your key competitor reduces prices by 20 percent;
   • the country goes into recession;
   • new technology makes our current product lines obsolete;
   • competitors merge to create a market with a few big players instead of lots of smaller ones;
   • new technology prices out our product lines;
   • the pound becomes increasingly strong; or even
   • nothing changes.

4. Focus on how the scenario outline will affect key factors such as technological change, corporate structure, product lines and so on. Build a detailed scenario around each of your key drivers – this is the creative part of the process – and look for ways to build on the opportunities and reduce the threats they present. Consider how you can use your strengths, and which weaknesses will make you most vulnerable. Look for business opportunities

and ideas for capitalizing on the scenario you have constructed. Let's say your scenario supposes that new technology will price you out of the market. Could you spearhead the new technological changes? Or could you find a new application for your existing products? Or a modification which will bring the price right down so that it remains competitive? Or a valuable feature that the new technology won't be able to provide?

Construct a story or narrative around your scenario. Suppose you are a customer going through the process of buying or using your product (with the new technology described in the scenario in place). Suppose you are a sales executive preparing a presentation under the conditions of the new corporate structure scenario. Suppose you are sitting down to plan a marketing campaign when your main competitor's prices have just plummeted.

5. Summarize all your scenarios and the impact they will have on your business, and use them to develop strategies. And explore the ideas you have generated which are valuable whatever the future holds.

Example

Scenarios are an everyday technique at RICOH in Japan, one of the leading manufacturers of office automation equipment. It gives top priority to creative research. RICOH's planners study probable customer needs in the future to decide what to research. They study social trends and developments in technology, and use these to construct scenarios such as *the office in the year 2005*. They construct a detailed narrative around this scenario, imagining, for example, what life would be like for a typical customer, and what technology they would be using during their working day. They use these scenarios as a source of ideas for potential new products, about ten to fifteen of which they pick for research each year.

Sensory Images

A s many of the creative techniques in this book demonstrate, looking at a problem from a new perspective is often the key to solving it. When your mind breaks out of its usual rut into new ways of thinking, you can tap into rich new creative resources. One of the techniques for doing this is to use your five senses to give you a new angle on the problem.

It really does help to be relaxed for this approach (for relaxation technique see *Unconscious intuitive techniques*, p. 176). Close your eyes. Take each of your senses in turn and generate sensory images about your problem. Ask yourself:

- What does it look like?
- How does it feel?
- What sound does it make?

Individual technique: problem solving/Idea generation

To open up your mind to new ideas, try activating different parts of your brain. This approach is all about using the five senses as creative triggers.

See also: Association.

- How does it smell?
- What does it taste like?

You may be thinking that this is all very well for a concrete problem such as developing a new product, but what about an abstract problem? What if your problem is that interest rates have gone up again? What's that supposed to smell like?

The point is that these sensory images aren't going to be the answer to all your problems in themselves, but they can spark off ideas by association. So long as you stay in the general area of the problem, you can come up with images that you can easily relate back to your problem. In the case of interest rates, you could think about the smell of the financial pages of the newspaper, or of your accounts office. Or the smell of the coffee as you sit round the board table late into the night working on the problem. Any strong images, especially ones which evoke feelings – such as the feeling of sitting up all night worrying about a problem – are useful stimulators.

Variations

Another option is to put more distance between you and the problem, and use your senses to summon up images that are unrelated to it. Then think about these images in relation to the problem and see if they spark off any ideas. Do this by relaxing and closing your eyes and then, taking one sense at a time, allow one or more images to flow into your mind. Think about the first strong taste that comes to mind, or the most striking or unusual thing you remember seeing recently.

Another option is to take any experience you've had, such as driving a car, being trapped in a lift, visiting a funfair or bathing the dog. Think about all the sensory stimulations of the experience. One way to do this is to draw a five senses mind map of the experience (see *Mind mapping*, p. 114). Then see how you can apply these sensory images to your problem.

Here's another variation. Think of ways in which you can directly apply the five senses to your problem. This works particularly well for generating new products or services, or improving existing ones. Suppose you want to come up with new ideas for office cleaning services:

- *Sight* – Make the offices look more attractive; supply fresh flowers or offer plant care as well as cleaning.
- *Sound* (or lack of it) – Use the quietest possible vacuum cleaners, and make a point of being as near silent as possible, so as not to disturb office workers. Don't even say "good evening" unless they speak to you first.
- *Touch* – What do most office workers touch most often? Their keypads. Why not offer a specialized computer cleaning service, including cleaning the mouse, using a mini-vacuum on the keypad and so on.
- *Taste* – Leave a bowl of mints in reception after you've finished cleaning, and one in each meeting room.
- *Smell* – Use air fresheners, and offer clients a choice of scents – let the occupants of each room choose their own scent.

Example

Suppose you are looking for radical ideas to improve your range of cookers. What sort of ideas and associations might you five senses give you? Here are some possible answers to the basic five questions, along with ideas they might generate. The ideas don't always relate directly to the sense that gave rise to them – that's fine. A good idea is a good idea.

- *What does it look like?* – Black or white, shiny enamel with stainless steel trim. Squared corners, taller than it is wide. Hob on top, oven underneath.
  Ideas – Expand the range of colors and trim materials. Put the oven and hob next to each other at work surface height so the

cooker is wider than it is high, and the oven is at a more practical height.

- *How does it feel?* – Smooth and cold when not being used, front is hot when oven is on.

  Ideas – Use materials which don't heat up when the oven or hob is on. Use material for oven door that changes color when oven is on.

- *What sound does it make?* – The sound of the fan when the oven is on, and the bleep of the timer.

  Idea – Develop a silent fan. Install a voice chip, which tells you when it is time to check the oven instead of just bleeping. It could perform a variety of other functions as well, such as telling you if you have left the oven or hob turned on but unused for more than a preset time.

- *How does it smell?* – Of nothing except when it is in use, when it smells slightly of the food being cooked in it.

  Idea – Include an option for releasing the smell from the oven when it is wanted – for cooking bread or Sunday roasts or winter stews – and shutting it off when the smells are less inviting.

- *What does it taste like?* – Metallic, presumably, and not pleasant.

  Idea – Include a salt dispenser on the side of the cooker for easy salting of vegetables and stews. This could be designed to stay dry so the salt doesn't clog up.

Six Thinking Hats

S ix thinking hats is a method of thinking about any problem which separates your thoughts, or those of the group, into different types of thinking – such as emotional, logical, creative and so on. De Bono identifies six different kinds of thinking, each of which he identifies by a different color, so you have white hat thinking, red hat thinking, black, yellow, green and blue hat thinking.

The point of this is to make sure that each kind of thinking is applied to the problem. Many of us find it difficult to think in certain ways; for example we are cautious planners and find it hard to be positive and optimistic. But if you put on the relevant metaphorical hat, you will find it easier to think positively.

And it has another key benefit too. In a group situation, six thinking hats reduce ego-problems and conflict. If you have, say, the intuitive hat on, you can put forward feelings without any rational

Group technique: problem solving/idea generation

This method was developed by Dr Edward de Bono in the early 1980s. It sets out a framework for thinking, which recognizes six different modes of thinking and increases clarity of thought by using only one at a time.

argument to support them. Under other circumstances this might leave you open to criticism and demands that you justify your position, but not if you are wearing the red (emotional) thinking hat.

The formality and artificiality of this system is, curiously, its strength. It makes the participants aware that they are playing a game, and they are therefore more inclined to stick to the rules. In a sense it isn't you talking, it's the hat. This removes a lot of opportunity for ego or personal friction.

The six hats

Let's have a look at the type of thinking that belongs to each hat. You'll notice that de Bono has picked colors that relate to the kind of thinking involved – yellow is happy, black is negative and so on – so it is quite easy to remember what kind of thinking is directed by each hat.

- *White hat thinking* – This is pure facts and figures. Looking at the data without making any judgements.
- *Red hat thinking* – Use this to express feelings, intuitive responses, hunches.
- *Black hat thinking* – The most negative hat. This is the logical hat of caution and devil's advocate. Wear the black hat to examine obstacles and reasons why the thing won't work.
- *Yellow hat thinking* – The hat of positive, optimistic thinking. This is a constructive thinking hat, which looks for benefits and reasons why the plan or project will work.
- *Green hat thinking* – This is the hat to use for the most creative thinking. It is the hat of alternatives, of provocative ideas, of change.
- *Blue hat thinking* – This is the hat for standing back and taking an overview. In this hat you look not so much at the subject but at the thinking itself. It is by wearing the blue hat that you can see that what is needed is some white hat thinking, for example.

Using the hats

De Bono isn't recommending that we should constantly switch from one hat to another. Most of the time we think normally, but the six thinking hats are there as a tool to use when it seems useful. The idea is that as many people as possible in the organization should be familiar with the tool, and it should become part of the culture, to be used in several ways in discussions or meetings. It might help to give some examples of how the method can be used:

- The chair of a meeting might say "I think we need some yellow hat thinking here." The participants switch into positive mode for a while, regardless of their individual views about the subject. This gets a fresh perspective on the problem, and encourages the more negative members of the group to look at things from a different perspective.
- You might ask someone to put a particular hat on for a while. Perhaps someone is taking a very logical view of a problem, which you feel has a strong emotional content – for example, they are discussing the cost benefits of redundancies and you are more concerned with the impact on morale. You might request that they put on the red hat for a few moments.
- Most people spend most of their time in black hat mode. A group leader might ask one or more people to switch to a different hat for a while. This can liberate people who might feel obliged to take the cautious view for fear of being blamed if they associate themselves with a riskier course of action.
- You might ask to put a hat on yourself. If, for example, you have a radical idea that you are a little embarrassed about because of its bizarre nature, you might say "I'd like to put on the green hat." This signals that you are putting forward a creative idea, but you are not attempting to apply logic, judgement or any other kind of thinking to it; you are simply throwing the idea into the ring, absolved of any requirement to justify it. Or you might say, "With my red hat on, I don't like this idea."

Again, you can express your viewpoint with no obligation to justify it.

- If you are planning a project or process, the group leader might decide to apply each different type of thinking in turn, as a whole group. To begin with, you might ask everyone to put on their white hats to assemble all the relevant facts and figures. Then you might work through the other hats in turn to be sure you have covered all the key angles.

- You can also use the six thinking hats on your own. You might be aware that you are getting bogged down in black hat thinking over something, constantly looking for the negative, and you might make a conscious decision to apply yellow hat thinking. Or you might put on each hat in turn.

Six thinking hats is a fascinating approach to thinking, both creative and analytical, and well worth exploring. If you want to try it, it is well worth reading de Bono's own book *Six Thinking Hats* (see Further reading, p. 189).

Storyboarding

A lthough it was Walt Disney who originally conceived the idea of storyboarding – now widely used throughout the film industry – it was one of his executives, Mike Vance, who refined the concept into the technique described here. Mike Vance joined Disney in the 1960s, and recognized that storyboarding had a much wider application than film making alone. In the late 70s he left to become a consultant, advising businesses on how to use storyboarding.

Storyboarding is a highly creative process for project management and problem-solving. You begin by defining the problem or project, and writing this on a *topic card* (see example) which you pin

---

Group technique: problem solving/idea generation

Walt Disney originally devised this approach for planning animated films. He created a series of illustrations depicting major scenes in the film, and then built up a story around each one to flesh out the plan. In its business application, storyboarding entails creating a board that sets out key concepts and then links them together.

See also: 7 × 7 technique, Brainstorming, Rice storm.

at the top of a cork board (or something similar). Then you create a storyboard by developing headings across the top of the board (generally written on index cards and pinned up). Next, you brainstorm around each *header card*, and pin up each of the ideas you generate under the relevant heading as a *subber card* (see Table below).

Storyboards have great benefits as a creative technique:

- Putting the ideas up on a board helps you to see the whole picture; you can see how the ideas interconnect and fit together, and they often help you cross-fertilize ideas between one set of sub cards and another.
- Storyboards help you to immerse yourselves in a project or problem, piggy-backing on ideas and seeing new possibilities or areas for attention.
- The storyboard can remain in place on the wall throughout the project or the problem-solving process, and can be copied down if anyone needs a portable copy.

The stages

There are two stages to storyboarding: creative thinking and critical thinking. The first stage is the process for creating the storyboard. This is best done in a group of between eight and twelve people, with a leader and a recorder. The technique used to generate the storyboard is *brainstorming* (see p. 37): all ideas are encouraged with no criticism or judgement of any ideas at this stage.

TOPIC CARD						
Header	Header	Header	Header	Header	Header	Header
Subber	Subber	Subber	Subber	Subber	Subber	Subber
Subber	Subber	Subber	Subber	Subber	Subber	Subber
Subber	Subber	Subber	Subber	Subber	Subber	Subber
Subber	Subber	Subber	Subber	Subber	Subber	Subber

1. Identify the overall problem or topic, and write it on a card. This is the topic card and should be pinned at the top of the board. The card might say "launching the new range" or "raising our profile among end users" or "streamlining the production process."

2. Next, pin up two standard header cards, which should appear on every storyboard. At the top left of the board (but below the level of the topic card) pin up a header saying *purpose*. At the other end of the board pin up the final header saying *miscellaneous*.

3. Brainstorm the *purpose* header, and list under it all the subbers you can think of. For example, if the topic is *streamlining the production process* you might include purpose subbers such as: *reduce costs, speed up production times, minimize technical breakdowns* and so on.

4. Now brainstorm all the other headers you think are relevant to the topic. These are the major issues you think are relevant to the project or problem. If the topic is *launching the new range* the other headers are likely to include such issues as: the launch event, production schedules, publicity, preparing systems, staff training, and so on. If you're not sure whether something is important enough to be a header or not, make it a header for the moment, and you can always relegate it to a subber later.

5. Next, take each header in turn and brainstorm all the ideas you can think of which should go under this header. So under your header *publicity* you might include subbers such as: television advertising, direct mail, "PS" on all delivery notes, in-store demonstrations.

About half an hour or so is generally long enough for a creative thinking session. After this, take a break and then return for the critical thinking session, which generally takes up to about an hour and a half.

1. Look at each header in turn and evaluate it. Why is the header on the board? Will the idea work? Consider whether the idea really belongs as a header or not. If not, either move it somewhere

else as a subber, or get rid of it. This may mean repositioning the subbers underneath it – just because the header has to go, it doesn't mean all the subbers under it necessarily have to.

2. Now go on to the subbers. A brainstorming session such as you have just held is intended to produce a high quantity of ideas, so you need to slim these down now to something more manageable. So go through all the subbers evaluating each one, and deciding whether it really belongs there. At the end of this process you have your storyboard.

Four types of storyboard

There are generally reckoned to be four main types of storyboard. Sometimes you will want to produce only a planning or an ideas board, or perhaps both. However, for a major project you will need to create each of these four storyboards in turn.

1. *Planning storyboard* – This is the first board you need to produce, and its headers should cover all the main areas related to the topic. It is the springboard for the other storyboards, and for the project as a whole.

2. *Ideas storyboard* – The second storyboard is the one where creative ideas are developed. If you're working on a major project which needs creative input, one of the headers on the planning board should relate to *generating ideas* or *guidelines for creative thinking* or something of the sort. This header would generally become the topic card for the ideas storyboard, and the subbers under it would become headers on the ideas storyboard. You may also decide to add other headers to this board, perhaps relating to solutions you have generated while brainstorming the subbers.

3. *Organization storyboard* – This is the storyboard that starts to put the project into action. It covers the key questions of *what* needs to be done, *when* each task should start, and *who* is going

to do it. The header cards for this storyboard will be the key tasks that make up the project.

4. *Communications storyboard* – Once you have established what needs to be done, when, and by whom, the next stage is to communicate it. This storyboard sets out the answers to the questions of *who* needs to know, *what* they need to know, *when* they need to know it, and *how* are they going to be told. The header cards will generally list the key tasks once again, but the subbers will differ from the organization board.

Synectics

T his highly creative approach to problem solving was devised by William Gordon on the premise that creative problem-solving is best achieved by using non-rational thought to reach a rational solution. It works well when you have a problem that has been proving hard to solve, or which you feel is going to need a radically creative approach. The word synectics comes from the Greek and means *bringing forth together*; the idea is that you can find links between seemingly unconnected things, and by putting them together you can find a solution.

Synectics is a bit like brainstorming with lots of other bits thrown in. It employs a range of techniques, particularly *analogies and metaphors*

Group technique: problem solving

Synectics is founded on the principle that since creativity is more closely related to the emotional than to the rational, people are more likely to be creative if they are thinking in an emotional way. This technique incorporates several others, particularly analogy, association and the excursion technique.

See also: Analogies and metaphorical thinking, Association, Brainstorming, Excursion technique.

(see p. 16), *association* (p. 21), and the *excursion technique* (p. 76), to help the mind make these connections between apparently unrelated things, ideas, people and so on. It does this in order to achieve a two-fold purpose:

- to make the strange familiar (which promotes learning); and
- to make the familiar strange (which promotes innovation).

The techniques used, and the way in which the synectics session is conducted, draw on the emotional and irrational functions of the mind, which William Gordon argued were more conducive to creative thought. He set out three fundamental assumptions on which he based synectics:

1. Our creativity increases once we understand the mental processes that determine our behavior.
2. The emotional and irrational components of creative behavior are more important than the intellectual and rational components.
3. We can all learn to harness these emotional and irrational elements.

The stages

The synectics process generally requires a group leader and about half a dozen other people, including the problem owner. The attitude of the group is important to the success of the process. As with brainstorming, it is important that everyone is open to free-thinking and apparent contradiction in order to maximize creativity. Although the basic technique used is brainstorming, it is brainstorming with a difference. In this case participants are encouraged to be critical at certain times, in order to harness the emotional response.

The role of the group leader is vital, since it is the leader who decides which techniques to employ when, and when to encourage criticism of ideas. The leader should be experienced in working with other creative techniques, in order to know when to bring them in to the process.

1. The first step is to identify the problem. This is the stage of making the strange familiar. First, state the problem as you perceive it. The problem should then be discussed and analyzed. The problem owner should explain why it is a problem, what solutions have been tried so far, and what they want to achieve as a result of this session. Once everyone understands the problem it should be defined in a problem statement. This part of the process probably doesn't need to take more than a few minutes.

2. The second stage is to make the familiar strange. The group now begins to brainstorm solutions to the problem, which the leader writes up on a board as in any brainstorming session. However, at any time it seems useful the leader can ask the group to use other techniques to help stimulate emotional, irrational and creative thinking about the problem. The most commonly used techniques to use are:

   • analogies and metaphors (finding an analogy for the problem);
   • association (free associating concepts and ideas and then looking for a relation with the problem); and
   • excursion technique (a visualized journey whose images are recorded and then used to find analogies with the problem).

You can also use *trigger words*, which are instructions to transform ideas into something else. For example, if the trigger word *empathize* is employed, the group members can interpret it in any way they choose: sympathize, imagine they are the subject, imagine the subject has human characteristics, be subjective and emotional about the subject. Some sample trigger words are shown in the box.

subtract add transfer empathize animate superimpose change scale substitute fragment isolate distort disguise contradict parody prevaricate hybridize symbolize mythologize fantasize repeat combine

This is the creative part of the exercise, and will take up to about an hour. During this stage all ideas are written up, but there is no requirement yet to arrive at a solution. However, the leader can encourage criticism of ideas (unlike a true brainstorming session) if the emotional reaction to this seems worthwhile.

3. The final stage is to relate the ideas generated back to the original problem, encouraging the group – and the problem owner in particular – to find a suitable solution. The group should then discuss any proposed solutions until the best one is identified.

Synectics in action

Let's say that one of your people is working on developing a new kind of printer which will take continuous A4 listing paper without perforated strips down the edges. The biggest problem is finding a mechanism for keeping the paper straight without the sprocket holes down the perforated strips.

In order to resolve this, you call together the development technician concerned plus five other people – two more technicians, a paper specialist, a major customer who is interested in this new product and your production manager.

To begin with, you state the problem and your development technician explains why it is such a knotty problem, and what the requirements are that the final product needs to meet. Between you, you produce a problem statement: *To produce a mechanism for feeding continuous A4 sheets through a printer without slipping, using no sprocket holes or perforated edges.*

Open the session proper by brainstorming possible solutions, encouraging everyone to suggest anything they can think of and piggy-back on each other's ideas. Record all these ideas on a flipchart.

If this doesn't produce a result, ask the group to think of analogies for feeding paper through a printer. They might suggest putting clothes through a mangle, or newspapers through a printing press, or pasta through a cutting machine. Now ask them to think of analogies from nature (this is known as bionics). They may suggest, for example, underwater lava flows, which push continuously through fissures in the sea bed. You could ask the group to work on any ideas they generate by applying trigger words. For example, you might instruct them to *exercise* the idea. Or to *multiply* it. Whatever trigger word you choose, they are free to interpret it as they wish.

You might try free association. Pick a word at random, perhaps one from earlier in the session, which is not directly associated with the problem. You might choose *volcano*. Go round the group asking the first person to free associate another word from this one, and then asking each person in turn to free associate a word from the one given by the person before them. Record all these words, and then ask the group to look for connections between these words and the problem. Brainstorm some more using these words.

Try the excursion technique. Ask everyone in the group to close their eyes and go on a visualized journey through a particular location – maybe a theme park. Give them ten minutes, and then ask them to record the images they saw on their journey. Ask each person in turn to share their key images with the group, and get everyone to look for analogies and connections between these images and the problem.

You should find that a creativity-fest of this kind will generate plenty of ideas for solving problems, and that as the session continues the group's creativity levels will escalate. The trick is to keep the momentum going, and to encourage everyone to use each other's ideas as a springboard. If the group begins to get stuck in a rut, that's the time to bring in a new technique.

Two Words Technique

This is a simple and fun technique for generating ideas or
solutions when you're stuck on a problem. All you have to
do is to reduce your problem or subject to two words, and
then list synonyms for each of these. Then put these synonyms together in new combinations. No two words mean exactly
the same thing; they all have different nuances at the least. So by
substituting new words in place of the original ones, you open up a
whole new range of creative stimulants.

The stages

1. First of all, think about your problem or challenge and find two
    words that sum it up. These two words might constitute a phrase
    but they don't have to. They simply have to express the problem.

Individual technique: problem solving/idea generation

This simple technique reduces the focus of your ideas to two
words, and then uses these words to stimulate new ideas.

See also: Forced relationship.

They might be *increase/sales*, *non-stick/textured*, *promote/discounts*, or *sack/George*.

2. Next, draw two columns and write one of your two words at the top of each.

3. Beneath each word, list all the words you can find which mean pretty much the same thing. Don't think about whether these words are applicable in the context of the original problem, just choose words which are synonyms in general. You can use a thesaurus to do this if you like.

4. Now combine your first word with each of the words in the other column in turn. See what ideas these new combinations generate.

5. Repeat this process using the second of your original two words in combination with each of the words in the first column.

6. Now you can go on to work through all the other combinations available, starting with the first synonyms from each column and so on. You might find, for example, that the original words *promote/discounts* might, when you work your way down the columns, give you the combination *augment/rebate*. This might spark off new ideas for promoting a discount. How about increasing the discount by one percent for every consecutive monthly order?

Example

Suppose your problem is that you need to recruit new staff to your department. The problem is that you need highly trained people and they are not easy to find. First, reduce your problem to two words – let's say *recruit people*. Now write down each of these words at the top of a column, and list synonyms underneath, as in the following Table.

recruit	people
employ	staff
engage	employees
hire	individuals
enlist	humans
appoint	mortals
commission	parties
entertain	characters
post	guys

As you can see, there are nine words in each column. That gives you a total of 81 possible combinations. That must be enough to generate some good ideas. Here are some possibilities:

- *appoint/individuals* – You could ask top people in your organization and others to network to find possible applicants.
- *employ/guys* – This could spark off the idea of fireworks (forgive the pun). How about sending a direct letter to top people who are already employed enclosing a sparkler and a note saying, "We're looking for bright sparks."
- *hire/guys* – You could use a headhunter.
- *commission/employees* – Announce to all your staff that anyone who introduces you to a potential employee will get a cash reward if that person is appointed.
- *entertain/parties* – Hold a party or special event and invite top people in the field so you can meet them; it's a simple step to start talking to them about joining the organization.

Unconscious Intuitive Techniques

T he unconscious mind is a powerful creative tool. It does not follow the same patterns of logic and rational thinking that we tend to follow consciously, so it is more open to creative thought. It is, after all, where our dreams come from. So it stands to reason that if we want to think creatively, we would do well to tap into this resource. The problem is, as we know from our dreams, that it tends to get carried away on its own path, and we have to learn how to direct it towards the particular problem we want solved.

All these techniques and approaches depend on the assumption that your mind holds the answer somewhere, you simply have to find a way to release it, or to recognize the pattern or connection that is the clue to it. These techniques are worth trying when you

---

Individual technique: problem solving

This is a collection of techniques that involve setting your mind to work without structured conscious involvement. The idea is that your unconscious mind is capable of coming up with the answers if you just leave it alone for a while.

See also: Conscious intuitive techniques.

feel sure that you know the answer, or are capable of finding a solution, but you can't quite see it at the moment.

Using your intuition

Intuition is one of the strongest waking experiences of our subconscious mind at work. Some of us place complete faith in our intuition; some of us mistrust or ignore it completely. Most of us fall somewhere between these two extremes, but tend to use our intuition less than we might. The reason is that using your intuition is a skill, but it is one that most of us never practice. So when it matters, we are reluctant to rely on our gut feelings.

In order to practice using your intuition, listen to your gut feelings. Make a conscious effort to recognize them. Before you open a letter, think about what you reckon might be inside. When the phone rings, pause for a second to think who it might be on the other end of the line. Before you talk to a customer, listen to your intuition about what outcome the meeting will achieve – will you close the deal, finalize the details, sort out the problem or whatever the conversation is about? Take note of what your intuition tells you, and see how often it is right. Learn to listen to it.

Intuition is an essential management tool, but it must almost always be combined with reasoned thought. When it comes to problem solving, let your intuition guide you, but once you find a solution see if you can work your way to it by reason and analysis as well. Research into what makes managers successful has found that intuition is an important tool. Many successful managers make gut decisions and then check them with logical analysis, or conversely use their intuition to check up on decisions or ideas reached through rational thought. In other words, they search for an answer until they find one which satisfies both the conscious and the unconscious process.

Intuition is also useful for finding solutions quickly. With practice, your intuition will be right almost as often as the more laborious analytical approach – which will still get it wrong sometimes.

Often speed is more important than the actual solution you arrive at, and in these cases it makes sense to rely on your gut feeling.

If you need persuading that you should use your intuition when it comes to creative problem solving, here are a few examples of successful intuitive thinking:

- Henry Heinz used the number 57 because it just came into his head. Heinz actually had far more than 57 varieties of food at the time.
- Sam Walton founded the retailing giant Wal-Mart on principles he arrived at purely by gut feeling. He felt certain that he could build a successful retailing chain by giving cut-rate prices and avoiding major cities. He also felt that it was important to treat employees like members of a big family.
- When microwave technology was first developed, the experts all said that there was no future for it as a cooking medium; people just didn't want it. George Foerstner of Amana Refrigeration, Inc felt otherwise. His intuition told him that if the price was right, people would buy microwave cookers. On the basis of this gut feeling he developed and marketed the first microwave ovens, and proved the experts wrong.

Relaxation

Our subconscious takes a back seat to our conscious thought processes when we are awake. So if the answer is there, it may not be apparent. We need to get our conscious minds to shut up for a moment. We need to calm down not only our rational thinking, but also our emotions. Negative emotions in particular, such as worry, anger and stress, inhibit our ability to listen to our subconscious.

The answer is to relax. Mental relaxation leads to more creative intuitive thought, and deep relaxation produces alpha brain waves which are conducive to intuitive thought (in our normal waking state our brains use the quicker, shallower beta waves). If the solution is already somewhere in your mind, you are more likely to see it in alpha state than in beta state.

There are several different relaxation techniques you can use; find the one that suits you best. Whichever you use you should be on your own in a peaceful environment, comfortable but able to sit for about a quarter of an hour with your eyes closed but without falling asleep. Then simply empty your mind, use the technique you have chosen, and allow your thoughts to drift. When you have finished, come round slowly – open your eyes, breathe deeply and slowly stretch your arms and legs – before going back to the fray. Here are a few techniques to try if you don't already have your own preferred one:

- Think about some occasion in the past when you have been relaxed and happy. Imagine this in detail, and try to recreate the sense of calm and relaxation. It might be lying on a beach in the sun, walking in the country, sitting in front of the fire with a mug of cocoa, or watching a sunset. Imagine this scene regularly; every day if possible, if only for three or four minutes. After a while, your mind will associate this with relaxation, and you will be able to use this technique to create a state of relaxation at will. Then you can empty your mind and allow your thoughts to drift.

- Try tensing and releasing every muscle in your body in turn. With your eyes closed, simply focus on tensing your toes and then releasing them slowly. Now tense your feet and then slowly release. Work your way slowly up your body – calves, knees, thighs, buttocks, lower back, stomach, upper back, chest, shoulders, upper arms, lower arms, hands, fingers, neck, head, face, eyes, forehead. As you progress, each part of your body that relaxes should stay relaxed. By the time you reach the end, you should be deeply relaxed and your mind should be empty.

- Breathe slowly in and out to a count of five each way allowing your ribcage to expand and contract but without moving your diaphragm. Now breathe in and out to a count of five using your diaphragm only – in other words, without allowing your ribcage to expand and contract. Finally, breathe in to a count

of five expanding your ribcage, and then breathe in further using your diaphragm to a count of five. Breathe out again with
your diaphragm first and then your ribcage. Repeat this whole
cycle – ribs in and out, diaphragm in and out, ribs then diaphragm in, diaphragm then ribs out – at least three times, or
until you feel deeply relaxed.

- Breathe slowly and deeply as you count backwards from fifty
down to one.

- Imagine a huge hot-air balloon on the ground in the middle of
a green field. Picture yourself placing all your anxieties, fears,
stress and negative feelings in the basket. Then untie the rope
that holds the balloon and watch it lift up, carrying away all
your unwanted emotions. Watch it until it disappears from view
beyond the horizon.

Don't assume that the answer will come to you immediately. It may
do, but then again sometimes it won't come at all. More often, you
will find at least some insight into the solution to your problem, even
if you don't find the whole solution. But it may not happen at once.
Perhaps later in the day, or the next time you relax, or the next time
you think logically about the problem, you will see a solution you
hadn't seen before.

This is a particularly good technique to use when it is the problem itself which is making you tense and stressed. Maybe you're
worrying about how to persuade a key client to accept an important
proposal, or perhaps your team members are falling out over a particular issue that you need to resolve.

Sleeping on it

How often have you struggled to remember the name of an actor –
or a movie, or the customer you met at that exhibition last month, or
the thing you forgot to write on your shopping list – only to have it
spring into your mind an hour or two after you've given up trying to
remember it?

Just because you are not consciously thinking about something, it doesn't mean you are not thinking about it subconsciously. Your subconscious is constantly processing ideas, images and information. This technique involves making sure that your subconscious is working on your particular problem rather than anything else. You want it to generate ideas to solve your problem so that next time you come back to it you see the solution. Sometimes the ideas will simply pop into your head while you're doing something else – just like the name of that actor.

Sleeping on it is not the only way to incubate ideas. (It was, however, Einstein's favorite method. If he encountered a really knotty problem, he used to take a nap.) It doesn't matter whether you go to sleep, go out for the evening, go into a tough meeting or take a bath. The only thing that matters is that you do something unconnected with the problem. But you have to prime your subconscious first:

- Immerse yourself in the problem for a while. Read any information about it. Think about it. Talk to your colleagues about it.
- Say to your subconscious: "OK, here's the problem. I need to find a way to make a shampoo bottle that stands up on its own, but *all* the shampoo comes out of it – even the last bit – without any hassle. Think about it, and let me know when you come up with an answer."
- Now stop thinking about the problem. Distract yourself if necessary. Either wait for inspiration to strike, or go back to the problem after a couple of hours, or a couple of days.

Tapping into your dreams

This is quite similar to sleeping on a problem, except that you are looking for the answer in your dreams rather than in a moment of conscious thought after you wake up. Many highly creative people keep dream diaries, in which they record their dreams; one of the most famous of these was the French philosopher Descartes. Other people too have been inspired by their dreams:

- Samuel Taylor Coleridge dreamed the poem *Kubla Khan*.
- Robert Louis Stephenson dreamed his novels before he wrote them.
- A model of the atom came to the physicist Niels Bohr in a dream.
- The arrangement of the elements was dreamt by Dmitri Mendeleyev.

These are just a few examples of the power of dreams. The question is, how do you harness that power? As with sleeping on a problem, you need to be clear exactly what the problem is that you are trying to solve. Formulate a question that expresses it clearly, and think about this before you fall asleep. Be prepared to do this for several nights in a row before you find the answer. After that, you need to remember your dreams:

- If you don't usually remember your dreams, wake up half an hour earlier than usual – this makes you more likely to wake during a period of dreaming. Before you open your eyes, concentrate on thinking through and remembering the dream, or you may well forget it when you get up.
- Keep a notebook beside your bed and record everything you can remember of the dream before you get up. You can write, sketch, or whatever helps you get the dream down.
- Now think about how the dream might relate to your problem. The answer may be direct or, more likely, indirect. You may need to free associate (see p. 21) with one or two images from the dream (use your intuition to decide which ones).
- Continue to record your dreams each morning. The more you do this, the more detail you will be able to remember.

Dreaming solutions to problems is usually indirect. You might dream a particular word or image that is a clue, rather than a clear answer.

For example, the inventor of the sewing machine, Elias Howe, was having trouble with the finer points of the design. One night he dreamed he was captured by savages carrying spears. The spears each had a hole in the tip. On waking, Howe realized that the modification he needed was to put the hole at the tip of the needle – the opposite end to the hole in an ordinary needle.

W hen you have a complex problem to solve, it is important to be sure that you cover every possible angle to solve it. One of the best ways to do this is with a checklist you can run through. Checklists can be made up of either single words or questions. There are plenty of standard ones around for different problems, or you can develop your own, perhaps by adapting an existing one.

One of the most important things about using checklists is that you must do it properly. It's no good skimming through the list; you need to spend time on every single item on the list – and a long time on some of them – for the technique to work. Although checklists are generally regarded as an individual tool, you can of course use them in a group. You could go through the list and identify the items that provoke most thought and then brainstorm these.

Individual technique: problem solving/idea generation

By going through a structured process – a checklist of words or questions – you can make sure you examine every aspect of a problem or every possible solution.

See also: Morphological analysis, Questions.

As you go through your checklist, alone or in a group, record the answers, notes and ideas you generate. If you don't find a solution, you should at least have made the problem clearer so you can go on and use another technique to solve it.

The Osborn verbal checklist

One of the most popular checklists of all time is the one devised by Alex Osborn, who also invented brainstorming. This is a checklist for finding improvements for a product or service. Osborn took nine verbs to apply to the product or service, and then added questions to expand on the ideas prompted by each of the nine words. The result is shown below.

Put to other uses?	New ways to use as is? Other uses if modified?
Adapt?	What else is like this? What other idea does this suggest? Does the past offer parallel? What could I copy? Whom could I emulate?
Modify?	New twist? Change meaning, color, motion, sound, odor, form, shape? Other changes?
Magnify?	What to add? More time? Greater frequency? Stronger? Higher? Longer? Thicker? Extra value? Plus ingredient? Duplicate? Multiply? Exaggerate?
Minify?	What to subtract? Smaller? Condensed? Miniature? Lower? Shorter? Lighter? Omit? Streamline? Split up? Understate?
Substitute?	Who else instead? What else instead? Other ingredient? Other material? Other process? Other power? Other place? Other approach? Other tone of voice?
Rearrange?	Interchange components? Other pattern? Other layout? Other sequence? Transpose cause and effect? Change pace? Change schedule?
Reverse?	Transpose positive and negative? How about opposites? Turn it backward? Turn it upside down? Reverse role? Change shoes? Turn tables? Turn other cheek?
Combine?	How about a blend, an alloy, an assortment, an ensemble? Combine units? Combine purposes? Combine appeals? Combine ideas?

From Applied Imagination, Alex Osborn, reproduced by permission of the Creative Education Foundation

Creating your own checklist

The second box contains a group of verbs you might apply to a product or service to find ideas for improving it. It is obviously not exhaustive, but you can add words of your own to these to create your own checklist.

multiply	divide	eliminate	subdue
invert	separate	transpose	unify
dissect	distort	rotate	flatten
squeeze	complement	submerge	freeze
harden	open up	melt	heat
soften	fluff up	bypass	add
subtract	widen	repeat	thicken
stretch	extrude	help	protect
fold	shake	smooth	color
segregate	integrate	symbolize	abstract

The Phoenix checklist

This checklist of questions was developed by the CIA to help agents examine a challenge or problem from every angle. It is a two-part checklist: first it explores the problem and then the plan for resolving it.

The problem

- Why is it necessary to solve the problem?
- What benefits will you receive by solving the problem?
- What is the unknown?
- What is it you don't yet understand?
- What is the information you have?
- What isn't the problem?
- Is the information sufficient? Or is it insufficient? Or redundant? Or contradictory?
- Should you draw a diagram of the problem? A figure?

- Where are the boundaries of the problem?
- Can you separate the various parts of the problem? Can you write them down? What are the relationships of the parts of the problem? What are the constants of the problem?
- Have you seen this problem before?
- Have you seen this problem in a slightly different form?
- Do you know a related problem?
- Try to think of a familiar problem having the same or a similar unknown
- Suppose you find a problem related to yours that has already been solved. Can you use it? Can you use its method?
- Can you restate your problem? How many different ways can you restate it? More general? More specific? Can the rules be changed?
- What are the best, worst and most probable cases you can imagine?

The plan

- Can you solve the whole problem? Part of the problem?
- What would you like the resolution to be? Can you picture it?
- How much of the unknown can you determine?
- Can you derive something useful from the information you have?
- Have you used all the information?
- Have you taken into account all essential notions in the problem?
- Can you separate the steps in the problem-solving process? Can you determine the correctness of each step?
- What creative thinking techniques can you use to generate ideas? How many different techniques?
- Can you see the result? How many different kinds of results can you see?
- How many different ways have you tried to solve the problem?
- What have others done?

- Can you intuit the solution? Can you check the result?
- What should be done? How should it be done?
- Where should it be done?
- When should it be done?
- Who should do it?
- What do you need to do at this time?
- Who will be responsible for what?
- Can you use this problem to solve some other problem?
- What is the unique set of qualities that makes this problem what it is and none other?
- What milestones can best mark your progress?
- How will you know when you are successful?

Verbal checklists in action

Let's say you manufacture kitchen equipment – blenders, mixers, juicers and so on. Several new competitors have recently entered the market, and competition is tougher than ever. Prices are being driven down, margins are slipping and you need to find ways to cut costs. Trouble is, you've been trimming them for months, you've renegotiated with all your suppliers, and you're running out of options. You need to come up with something radical.

Try applying a few verbs from your checklist at random. Here in the table are three examples, and the ideas they might generate.

Color	Suppose you reduce the number of finishes and colors your products come in? At the moment, most have at least three options. Cut this to two and you'd cut costs, without necessarily damaging sales.
Bypass	How about selling direct to customers as well as through retailers? Bypass the middle person with a mail order arm of the business, and you could increase your margins substantially.
Protect	What about packaging? All that bubble-wrap to protect your goods in transit is expensive. Maybe you could develop low-cost packaging that still prevents breakages.

Further Reading

101 Creative Problem Solving Techniques, James M. Higgins, The New Management Publishing Company, Winter Park, FL, 1994.

A Whack on the Side of the Head, Roger von Oech, Warner Books, New York, 1998.

Applied Imagination, Alex Osborn, Creative Education Foundation, Buffalo, NY, 1963.

Brain Boosters for Business Advantage, Arthur B. VanGundy, Pfeiffer & Company, San Diego, CA, 1995.

Cracking Creativity: The Secrets of Creative Genius, Michael Michalko, Ten Speed Press, Berkeley, CA, 1998.

Creative Whack Pack, Roger von Oech, United States Games Systems, Stamford, CT, 1989.

Instant Creativity, Brian Clegg & Paul Birch, Kogan Page, London, 1999.

Lateral Thinking: Creativity Step-By-Step, Edward de Bono, HarperCollins, London, 1973.

Six Thinking Hats, Edward de Bono, Little, Brown & Co, New York, 1985.

The Mind Map Book, Tony Buzan, Plume Books, New York, 1996.

Think out of the Box, Mike Vance & Diane Deacon, Career Press, Franklin Lakes, NJ, 1995.

Thinkertoys, Michael Michalko, Ten Speed Press, Berkeley, CA, 1991.

Use Both Sides of Your Brain, Tony Buzan, Plume Books, New York, 1991.

Axon Idea Processor, Axon Research – This is a sketchpad for visualizing and organizing ideas, creating mind maps, text processing, checklists, hints and problem solving.

CK Modeller, IDON Software – A graphics-based program for recording and manipulating ideas using shapes.

Corkboard/Three by Five, MacToolKit – This allows you to storyboard using virtual index cards on a bulletin board.

Creative Whack Pack, Creative Think Software – This is the electronic version of the Creative Whack Pack (see *Further Reading*). Give the program a problem and it will show you randomly selected cards and questions to stimulate your creative processes.

IdeaFisher, Fisher Idea Systems – A sophisticated program for brainstorming and problem solving, this helps you generate solutions for problems such as marketing strategies, articles, advertising and promotion, and generating names for things.

Innovation Toolbox, Infinite Innovations Ltd, UK – This program uses many techniques such as random input, the Osborn verbal checklist, brainstorming, analogies and many others, all within a problem solving structure.

MindMan, MindMan Infocentre – An easy and quick way to create mind maps with graphic features; you can easily change the mind map using drag and drop, and choose your preferred format to print it.

Serious Creativity, Meta4 Software – A computer-based training package based on Edward de Bono's *Six Thinking Hats* system.

Useful Web Sites

The Creativity Web – www.ozemail.com.au/~caveman/Creative – This aims to be the most up-to-date resource center for creativity and innovation on the Internet. It is packed with information about books, software, people, organizations, quotations, techniques, the brain and more.

Directed Creativity– www.directedcreativity.com: This site has a comprehensive collection of creativity techniques.

Edward de Bono – www.edwdebono.com – This gives information on most of de Bono's work in the teaching of creativity including *Six Thinking Hats* and lateral thinking.

The Innovation Network – www.thinksmart.com – Numerous articles on personal creativity and organizational innovation in the article archives.

What a Great Idea! – www.whatagreatidea.com – The Web site of Charles 'Chic' Thompson, author of *What a Great Idea* and *Yes But*. Full of ideas on how and where to get ideas, and how to overcome resistance to them.

Enchanted Mind – www.enchantedmind.com – A colorful, well-designed site with a great deal of information on creativity techniques as well as articles, puzzles and humor.

Index